Cambridge Elements ≡

Elements in Public and Nonprofit Administration
edited by
Andrew Whitford
University of Georgia
Robert Christensen
Brigham Young University

CRITICAL RACE THEORY

Exploring Its Application to Public Administration

Norma M. Riccucci
Rutgers University, Newark

CAMBRIDGE
UNIVERSITY PRESS

Critical Race Theory

Exploring Its Application to Public Administration

Elements in Public and Nonprofit Administration

DOI: 10.1017/9781009122986
First published online: February 2022

Norma M. Riccucci
Rutgers University, Newark
Author for correspondence: Norma M. Riccucci, riccucci@rutgers.edu

Abstract: This Element explores Critical Race Theory (CRT) and its potential application to the field of public administration. It proposes specific areas within the field where a CRT framework would help to uncover and rectify structural and institutional racism. This is paramount given the high priority that the field places on social equity, the third pillar of public administration. If there is a desire to achieve social equity and justice, systematic, structural racism needs to be addressed and confronted directly. The Black Lives Matter (BLM) movement is one example of the urgency and significance of applying theories from a variety of disciplines to the study of racism in public administration.

Keywords: social equity, institutional racism, structural racism, Black Lives Matter, White supremacy

ISBNs: 9781009114165 (PB), 9781009122986 (OC)
ISSNs: 2515-4303 (online), 2515-429X (print)

Contents

There must exist a paradigm, a practical model for social change that includes an understanding of ways to transform consciousness that are linked to efforts to transform structures.

hooks 1995, *Killing Rage: Ending Racism*

Introduction

Critical Race Theory (CRT) is a framework that adopts a race-conscious approach to uncover and better understand institutional and structural racism in our society with the aim of promoting and achieving social justice. The premise of CRT is that our legal, political, and economic institutions are inherently racist and that race is a socially constructed concept that enables and justifies the ability of Whites to promote their own economic, social, and political interests at the expense of people of color (Bell, 1992, 1995; Crenshaw, 1988).[1] Bell and other legal scholars advanced the theory in the 1970s and 1980s in response to the lack of or incremental progress being made by the civil rights movement, arguing that White liberal ideals such as equal opportunity, freedom of choice, and merit advanced the interests, privileges, and entitlement of Whites while perpetually repressing and oppressing people of color.

Initially relied upon in legal studies as a framework to analyze patterns in law, court cases, and legal precedents, CRT more recently has been applied to a number of disciplines, including sociology (Bonilla-Silva, 2015; Ray et al., 2017; Romero, 2001), social work (Moore et al., 2018), criminology (Coyle, 2010; Cunneen and Tauri, 2019; Schneider, 2003), social psychology (Correll et al., 2007; Kang et al., 2012), public health (Gilbert and Ray, 2016), and predominantly education (Banks, 1995; Garcia, López, and Vélez, 2017; Ladson-Billings, 1999; Sablan, 2019).[2] Research has employed both qualitative and quantitative methodologies, although a number of provisos have been advanced around the application and suitability of quantitative methods.

This Element addresses these issues in the context of public administration research, and proposes areas within the field that could benefit from the application of a CRT framework. This requires a shift in the field, which is desirable

---

[1] Critical theory in a broad sense focuses on structural and institutional barriers (e.g., social and economic) that persons face based on social identity. It accepts the premise that putatively neutral or impartial norms are inherently biased, thus limiting the applicability of "traditional" theories. Critical theories have been applied in public administration as will be seen later in the text (see, e.g., Stivers, 1991). Also see, later in the text, Blessett's (2020) application of CRT to urban renewal efforts in Baltimore, Maryland.

[2] As Hochschild (2005) observes, few political scientists tend to rely on a CRT framework. In addition, as she goes on to say, they do not spend much time "thinking about the linguistic connotations of or conceptual boundaries around 'race' or 'ethnicity,' or much time debating the legitimacy of categories such as Black, Latino, or Asian. Most simply use the terms as either independent or dependent variables depending on the nature of their analysis" (p. 108).

given the high priority that the field places on social equity, the third pillar of public administration (Frederickson, 1990; Gooden, 2014). If there is a desire to achieve social equity and justice, racism needs to be addressed and confronted directly. The Black Lives Matter (BLM) movement is one example of the urgency and significance of applying theories from a variety of disciplines to the study of racism in public administration.

Critical Race Theory

Derrick Bell and other legal scholars, including Kimberlé Crenshaw,[3] Richard Delgado, Patricia Williams, and Mari Matsuda, advanced CRT to address the pervasive problem of racism in our society, which they argued is ubiquitous throughout America's institutions. CRT is a theoretical framework that centers around the experiences and needs of people of color, particularly Black and Brown people; it challenges dominant frameworks and ideologies that are White-centered, White normative, or White supremacist in origin. A basic tenet of CRT is that racism, race, and its intersections with other identity markers, such as gender, sexuality, and class, are an endemic part of society and are institutionalized in and by the law and public policy. CRT maintains that racism is not limited to individual acts or interpersonal bigotry, but rather, it is structural and systemic and accomplished by laws, legal reforms, and public policy, which may be unintentional, but are cloaked in choices that are racist (Bonilla-Silva, 2015; Crenshaw et al., 1995; López et al., 2018; Matsuda, 1987; Williams, 1987). Bell and others, for example, argued that racism permeated civil rights laws in housing and employment, whereby housing transactions and employment criteria were racist in practice – and still are – even though they may not have been racist in intent. The continued reliance on "merit" in hiring and promotion exams in the public sector, which has a disproportionately harsh impact on persons of color, is an example here (Portillo, Bearfield, and Humphrey, 2020). Another example can be seen in the continuance of racially segregated schools – almost seventy years after *Brown* v. *Board of Education* (1954) outlawed school segregation. CRT studies embrace race consciousness and seek to alter how race and racism were conceived in White America's consciousness. It challenges the pretense that racism does not exist, that merit or incompetence, excellence, or inferiority could explain away racism and racial imbalance. CRT unravels the American myth.

Bell (1995: 899), a pioneer in CRT studies, has argued that critical race theorists "are highly suspicious of the liberal agenda, distrust its method, and want to retain what they see as a valuable strain of egalitarianism which may

---

[3] Crenshaw is credited with coining the term, "Critical Race Theory."

exist despite, and not because of, liberalism." He goes on to say that there are healthy tensions in CRT scholarship, "between its commitment to radical critique of the law (which is normatively deconstructionist) and its commitment to radical emancipation by the law (which is normatively reconstructionist)," or as we can deduce, between merely exposing the hidden fallacies of law – or in common parlance, trashing the law – and reconstructing or reshaping racial structures through legislation. For CRT scholars, law is never neutral and each successive wave of reform legislation works to reinforce racial hierarchies; advances for Blacks through reform bills come only when the interests of Whites are served, according to critical legal theorists.

Early on, areas that legal scholars examined in the context of CRT included the concept of colorblindness and affirmative action. Bell (1995: 899), for example, argued that policies such as affirmative action do not address the underlying problem of institutional and structural discrimination in our society. We could eliminate the need for affirmative action if we eradicated discrimination and racism. Bell (1989: 1598) questions the effectiveness of affirmative action, arguing that the policy is "the latest contrivance the society has created to give blacks the sense of equality while withholding its substance." In fact, Bell (1989: 1602) suggests that affirmative action policies are intended to benefit Blacks only to the extent that their gains do not threaten or impinge upon the status or "property interests" of Whites. He goes on to say that

> [t]hose who wield effective control in the nation make, when considered necessary, that amount of social adjustments that will help to siphon off sufficient discontent to enable the societal status quo to be maintained. ... [T]oken or cosmetic gains are extended under the formal Constitution, while, under the operational code, of the unwritten basic law, no real redistribution of wealth, prestige, or social power takes place (Bell, 1989: 1598–1599).

Parenthetically, years later Bell (2000: 145) admitted that "[n]o one can say that affirmative action has failed. Over the years and despite the controversy and widespread opposition, a substantial number of African Americans, most certainly including this author, and many other people of color owe their success at least in part to the functioning of affirmative action policies." These policies, he states, helped to increase diversity in government agencies and businesses. However, he goes on to say that affirmative action has been far more helpful to White women.

Also a pioneer in CRT scholarship, Crenshaw (1988, 1996) points to tensions within CRT legal scholarship. For example, she suggests that some CRT scholars do not adequately consider the development of strategies for change that include the pragmatic use of legal rights. She argues that legal rights are the means by which oppressed groups have secured both entry as formal equals into the dominant order and the survival of their movement in the face of private and state repression. The dual role of legal change creates a dilemma for Black reformers. As long as race consciousness thrives, Blacks will often have to rely on rights rhetoric when it is necessary to protect Black interests. The very reforms brought about by appeals to legal ideology, however, seem to undermine the ability to move forward toward a broader vision of racial equality. In the quest for racial justice, winning and losing have been part of the same experience (Crenshaw, 1988: 1385). Eradicating racial domination, she maintains, requires nullifying the hegemonic function of racism and chipping away at the premises of the continuing ideology of white race consciousness. Legal reforms that do not repackage racism are part of the solution that can ultimately help to restore the traditions and cultures of Black, Brown, and Indigenous people before they are forced to integrate and assimilate into the White society.

Crenshaw and colleagues (1995) point out that CRT was conceived by scholars of color, mostly in law schools, who challenge the manner in which race and racial power are constructed and represented in American legal culture as well as American society as a whole. According to CRT scholars, although race is socially constructed and does not stem from natural differences, it produces negative effects in our society. As Banks (1995: 22) points out, race is "a human invention constructed by groups to differentiate themselves from other groups, to create ideas about the 'Other,' to formulate their identities and to defend the disproportionate distribution of rewards and opportunities within society."[4]

And, although there is no canonical set of doctrines or methodologies to which all CRT scholars subscribe, there are two common interests in CRT scholarship (Crenshaw et al., 1995: xiii). One is to explicate how White supremacy has created and maintained institutions and systems that subordinate people of color, particularly through White liberal ideals of law and equal protection. The second common interest is the goal of transforming the inextricable linkage between law and racial power, to ultimately promote an ethos of human liberation.

In the last two decades or so, CRT studies have moved to disciplines well beyond law, to include sociology, education, social psychology, and criminology.[5] In this sense, CRT can be seen as transdisciplinary in that

---

[4] Also see Omi and Winant (2015), who refer to the social construction of race as the "racial formation process," whereby political, social, and economic forces determine the content, meaning and significance of racial categories.

[5] In terms of practice, the political right has been critical of CRT, arguing that it is divisive and a "left-wing myth." To some white people it is too discomforting – or irritating – to hear how

researchers from various disciplines continue to work toward creating new conceptual, theoretical, and methodological advances to move beyond discipline-specific approaches to the universal, persistent problem of racism. Research applying CRT in all of these disciplines seeks to eradicate racism as part of a larger goal to eliminate oppression in all forms in our society and at every intersection (Matsuda, 1991; Matsuda et al., 1993; Sung and Coleman, 2019).[6] The CRT research thus far has relied more on qualitative than on quantitative methods.

Critical Race Methodology

CRT is an ontological and epistemological framework with which to analyze racism and racial inequities. Seminal studies in CRT, as noted, derived from law and examined the intersection of race with gender in antidiscrimination laws with a focus on White supremacy and structural racism in legal progresses (Crenshaw, 1996; Delgado and Stefancic, 1993, 2017; Sablan, 2019). CRT was primarily viewed as a method of legal analysis where the development and implementation of laws was a means to subordinate racial groups (Brown, 2003; Crenshaw, 1996). Thus, early on critical race methodology (CRM) was imperatively qualitative and steeped in a Realist tradition. Indeed, critical legal theory emanated from the Realist movement, wherein law is viewed as neither value-free nor neutral and is inextricably entwined with politics and social issues. Today, CRT research is both qualitative and quantitative, although traditional critical race theorists advanced a number of provisos around the application and suitability of quantitative methods, as will be seen shortly. Ultimately, the suitability of a CRM will certainly depend upon the topic of study and the research questions asked.

White supremacy has created racist structures and institutions in America (see work on White fragility). Despite the fact that CRT is not taught in K-12 classrooms or in high schools, a number of Republican-led bills across the country in the 2020s have sought to ban the teaching of CRT in classrooms. A Rhode Island bill, for example, disparages the idea that "the United States of America is fundamentally racist or sexist" (Adams, 2021: online). And in September of 2020, Trump directed his Office of Management and Budget (OMB) to ban its use throughout the federal government, despite the fact that it was not in use: "All agencies are directed to begin to identify all contracts or other agency spending related to any training on 'critical race theory,' 'white privilege,' or any other training or propaganda effort that teaches or suggests either (1) that the United States is an inherently racist or evil country or (2) that any race or ethnicity is inherently racist or evil" (OMB Memorandum, 2020: online). It seems that many have no clear conception of what CRT really is or does. In June of 2021, President Biden rescinded Trump's ban on diversity training. Dog whistles and obscurantist conceptions of CRT advanced by the right wing have sought to sidetrack the issues, but their repudiation seems more like an effort by White people to hold on to their power.

[6] CRT and CRMs are also able to address the inequities at the micro (individual), meso (organizational), and macro (societal) levels. See text later in this Element where the work of Victor Ray is addressed.

The Qualitative Case

Qualitative research has been the dominant form in CRT studies, and, in fact, many critical race theorists maintain that, because of their ability to understand and contextualize the nuances of everyday experiences and the social processes that result in racism, qualitative approaches are the most suitable. These traditional critical race theorists have argued that quantitative methods are antithetical to the core tenets of CRT. They argue, for example, that quantitative research presumes objectivity and neutrality, which contradicts tenets that take a definitive stance on the role of race and racism in our society Carbado and Roithmayr, 2014; Garcia, López, and Vélez, 2017; Sablan, 2019; Smith, 2012). Their main concern here is that race poses challenges to objective judgments in the United States (Sablan, 2019; Smith, 2012). Moreover, researchers cannot separate themselves from what they observe. According to Garcia, López, and Vélez (2017: 151), the main arguments against quantitative methods in CRT studies include the following:

(1) The centrality of racism as a complex and deeply rooted aspect of society that is not readily amenable to quantification

(2) The acknowledgment that numbers are not neutral and they should be interrogated for their role in promoting deficit analyses that serve White racial interests

(3) The reality that categories are neither "natural" nor given and so the units and forms of analysis must be critically evaluated

(4) The recognition that voice and insight are vital: data cannot "speak for itself," and critical analyses should be informed by the experiential knowledge of marginalized groups

(5) The understanding that statistical analyses have no inherent value but they can play a role in struggles for social justice (also see Gillborn, Warmington, and Demack, 2018).

Sablan (2019: 181) argues that qualitative methods may be most appropriate because "Social science research on the whole is regarded by some as not fully equipped to reflect oppressed communities, including indigenous and colonized populations" (also see Smith, 2012). She rationalizes this by examining some of the aforementioned tenets, particularly with respect to the lack of objectivity in research. She goes on to say that quantitative methods tend to rely on positivistic paradigms, but qualitative methods may be better suited for critical theories and alternative epistemologies. Nonetheless, she concludes by opining that "critiquing the limits of post-positivism does not negate the potential use of [quantitative methods]" (Sablan, 2019: 181).

Experiential knowledge is central, legitimate, and appropriate for capturing
racial subordination. Thus, CRMs have included storytelling, biographies, family
histories, and narrative inquiry (see, Bell, 1987; Delgado, 1995; Williams, 1991).
CRM allows for research that is grounded in the experiences and knowledge of
people of color. Solórzano and Yosso (2002) make a distinction between traditional
storytelling and narratives, which they refer to as "master narratives." The former,
they argue, do not fully capture the complexities of and richness of a group's
cultural life, but rather portray and promote racial characterizations and stereotypes. They offer, instead, the concepts of counternarratives and counter-
storytelling. Solórzano and Yosso (2002: 32) define the counter-story as "a method
of telling the stories of those people whose experiences are not often told (i.e., those
on the margins of society). The counter-story is also a tool for exposing, analyzing,
and challenging the majoritarian stories of racial privilege."

Counter-stories refute racist characterizations of social life and seek to
expose "race neutral" discourse to reveal how white privilege operates to
augment inequities in race relations. As Manglitz, Guy, and Hunn (2006: online)
argued,

> [w]hile majoritarian stories draw on the tacit knowledge among persons in the
> dominant group . . ., they also distort and silence the experiences of the domin-
> ated. Counter-stories facilitate social, political, and cultural cohesion, as well as
> survival and resistance among marginalized groups. By acknowledging subju-
> gated discourses we not only recognize there is more than one way to view the
> world, but we also open up possibilities for understanding phenomena in new
> and different ways (also see Delgado and Stefancic, 2000; López, 2001).

Notwithstanding, traditional storytelling or narratives continue to dominate
CRT studies. Romero (2008), for example, relies on narrative in her CRT race
and immigration study. She begins by pointing out that mainstream sociological
research on immigration continues to focus on questions concerning assimila-
tion, acculturation, generational conflict, and social mobility. She argues that
the application of CRT allows for research to address more relevant and
contemporary issues such as racial profiling, anti-immigration bias, and the
increased militarization of the US–Mexico border. Her narrative on civil rights
violations of Mexicans by the Chandler, Arizona Police Department, and the
Tucson Border Patrol is illustrative. The Southwest Supermarket located in
Chandler was targeted by the police and border control for "citizen" inspection
of its patrons. Officers requested that the store's assistant manager, Ms.
Rodriguez, announce over the loudspeaker that all illegal aliens who were
shopping should turn themselves over to law enforcement officers in the parking
lot. Rodriguez refused, so the police and border patrol set up a command center
in the parking lot near the store and began following and stopping all customers

who appeared Mexican, asking for identification or proof of citizenship; White customers were not profiled. Romero (2008: 30–31) writes about a particular incident:

> A man with two small children, about three to four years of age, was contacted by officers as he walked out of the store. The man talked to the officers as he walked to his truck. He opened the door on the passenger side of the truck and placed his children in the vehicle. He then walked around the truck to the driver's side. At this time a Border Patrol officer approached the passenger door and placed the wheel of his bicycle behind the door to prevent it from being closed. A Chandler police officer placed his bicycle wheel behind the driver's door in a similar fashion. The Chandler officer talked to the man for a few minutes, then began to try to pull him from the truck cab. The Border Patrol officer then rounded the cab and helped the Chandler officer. They pulled him from the cab, handcuffed him and placed him in a police van. The children were crying and very upset. An officer returned to the truck in about five minutes, stayed there for some time, then made a phone call. Later, another officer arrived and removed the children. In the meantime, a woman customer went to the truck and tried to comfort the children. They were left in the truck for a total of 15 or 20 minutes.

Romero uses this narrative to depict how a Latinx elder was demeaned, humiliated, and subordinated in front of his children and other customers in the parking lot. Solely based on his physical appearance, the young children witnessed that their father was placed at risk before the law, and was treated as inferior compared to White customers. She goes on to say that "[a]lthough citizens who leave children in cars in the summer can be prosecuted for child endangerment, this man's children were left by the officers in July's triple-digit temperature without apparent concern for their safety or fear of legal action against them" (Romero, 2008: 31).

Although many critical race theorists argue that qualitative approaches such as those described earlier are more suitable for studies on race and ethnicity, others have more recently pointed to the need for quantitative studies. The qualitative–quantitative debate in CRT scholarship mirrors debates in feminist epistemology. For example, feminist theory maintains that statistical procedures in examining gender sex differences are inadequate as they rely on crude and simplistic data-labelling, which ignores the complexity of women's experiences (hooks, 1981, 2000; Roberts, 1981). Gender is a social construct, with identities that include, for example, "Agender," "Two Spirit," "Gender Expansive," "Intersex," "Transgender," and "Nonbinary/Genderqueer/Genderfluid." Moreover, feminist researchers contend that methodology is gendered in that quantitative methods have traditionally been associated with concepts such as positivism, scientific, objectivity, statistics, and masculinity (Oakley, 1998; Westmarland, 2001). But qualitative methods are associated with interpretivism, nonscientific, subjectivity, and femininity. Some feminist researchers have thus rejected quantitative methods as not aligning with the aims of feminist theory and research (see, e.g., Pugh, 1990; Reinharz, 1992). As Westmarland (2001: online) has pointed out, however, "different feminist issues need different research methods, and that as long as they are applied from a feminist perspective there is no need for the dichotomous 'us against them,' 'quantitative against qualitative' debates." Thus, a pluralistic approach seems suitable for CRT studies, particularly in the social sciences. And, in fact, a number of scholars have applied quantitative methods to CRT studies, despite the challenges advanced.

The Quantitative Case

A number of CRT scholars who support the application of quantitative methods to CRT studies, nonetheless, offer caveats or provisos in so doing (e.g., Garcia, López, and Vélez, 2017; Gillborn, Warmington, and Demack, 2018; López et al., 2018; Sablan, 2019). Indeed, many of the CRT studies that claim to be quantitative merely outline the problems associated with efforts to apply quantitative methods, particularly around measurement (e.g., deracializing statistics and developing measures for structural and institutional racism, as will be discussed in a later section).

The Caveats

"QuantCrit" refers to critical race theorists who promote or use quantitative methods but through self-reflection and avoiding the perpetuation of racist narratives through data (Cross, 2018).[7] A fundamental premise of QuantCrit is that statistics are socially constructed. In addition, because direct measures of racism are difficult to capture, as open, overt admission of racial bias has become less acceptable over time, indirect measures such as perceived racism and/or discrimination are relied upon. From this perspective, they have outlined key tenets for using statistical methods to advance social justice and equity. Mainly, they argue that an ontological shift is in order whereby quantitative CRMs account for the axiological underpinnings of social statistics, which they argue are racialized (see, Garcia, López, and Vélez, 2017). In other words, as Zuberi and Bonilla-Silva (2008) argue, quantitative CRT studies must account for the "white logic" in quantitative research (e.g., the lack of neutrality and objectivity). Covarrubias and Vélez (2013) and Vincent-Ruz (no date) offer the following:

---

[7] QuantCrit has been predominantly used, thus far, in the field of education.

1. Avoid using race as a variable that reifies race as a biological construct, which emanated from the White supremacist eugenics movement after emancipation in the United States (see Zuberi, 2001).
2. Include variables that focus on structure and institutions, in order to avoid focusing solely on individual factors.
3. Focus on malleable factors where interventions can produce change.
4. Consider a mixed-methods approach.
5. Acknowledge that we cannot separate analysis from the analyst.
6. Acknowledge that the disciplinary contexts in which we operate are primarily defined and led by White scholars.

Garcia, López, and Vélez (2017) call for a "deracialization" of statistics by challenging eugenicist assumptions about intelligence that frame Black communities as innately self-destructive and inferior. Indeed, these ideas are the centerpiece of the 1899 seminal work of W. E. B. Du Bois, *The Philadelphia Negro*. His mixed-methods study provided a counter-story to the prevailing traditional, eugenicist approach to studying social inequalities in Black communities in Philadelphia in the late 1800s and early 1900s. Du Bois (2007) provided a radical contextualization of the structural origins of social inequalities and demonstrated that structures of power operated to oppress Black communities (also see, Chapman and Berggren, 2005; Zuberi, 2000, 2001).

Deracializing statistics is challenging as it requires deracializing the social conditions that produce racialized inequalities.[8] Also, there is a good deal of ambiguity around the definition and conceptualization of deracializing. In effect, most researchers then simply assert explicitly that current methodologies fail to adequately account for the socially constructed nature of race. An example often offered here is when researchers adopt a conceptualization of race as a fixed attribute; but, as critical race theorists maintain, race cannot be considered fixed at birth, because this would antecede subsequent life outcomes, such as income or education, which are social circumstances that contribute to the social construction of race. Thus, the narrative by researchers then shifts to fundamental problems in constructing and measuring race as well as racism. Indeed, disciplines have acknowledged the lack of clarity around the use of racial variables

---

[8] Moreover, it has taken on different, almost opposing meanings depending upon the topic of study. For example, political scientists studying elections have constructed deracialization as downplaying racial themes to attract white voters, and defusing the polarizing effects of race by avoiding reference to race-specific issues. In an effort to gain white support, Hamilton (1973), for instance, indicated that blacks should address social issues that appeal to society as a whole. For Hamilton, one such issue was "full employment," rather than topics such as welfare or set-asides (also see Johnson, 2017). However, some have criticized such a race-neutral approach as marginalizing race itself, by subsuming black demands and interests for the sake of Whites (see, e.g., Rho'Dess, 2011).

within their respective fields. Race is not consistently conceptualized or measured across studies or disciplines, and the processes of operationalization are not always well documented. To be sure, these issues represent significant challenges for the validity and value of research results (Hanna et al., 2020).

Some scholars suggest that quantitative studies must consider structural factors such as institutional policies and societal norms that result in racial inequities. So, for example, as García and Sharif (2015) advise, because racism is a social condition and a fundamental cause of health and illness, epidemiologists must take into account indirect measures such as the significance of poverty. In addition, Zuberi (2000: 177) points out that in the context of causal inferences, the education a student receives can be a cause of the student's performance on a test, but the student's race, ethnicity, or gender cannot. He offers this example:

> [B]eing an African American should not be understood as the cause of a student's performance on a test, despite the fact that being African American can be a very reliable basis for predicting test performance. The logic of causal inference itself should give every nonpartisan scholar reason to avoid flamboyant rhetoric about the genetic-based cognitive causes for racial and gender stratification (also see Holland, 1986).

Darling-Hammond's (2007) commentary on No Child Left Behind (NCLB) points to failures in considering structural and institutional inequities in studies that assessed the efficacy of NCLB. Recall that the NCLB law held schools accountable for how children in the United States learned and achieved. Its goal was to raise the educational achievement of all children and to close the racial/ethnic achievement gap. The law was controversial for a number of reasons, particularly because of inequitable educational funding across the states and a shortage of highly trained teachers willing to serve in high-need schools (also see, Gillborn, Warmington, and Demack, 2018). As Darling-Hammond argued, under NCLB, the wider structural inequities that shape educational outcomes were ignored because attention was focused on the *school* level. But, as she points out,

> the wealthiest US public schools spend at least 10 times more than the poorest schools. . . . Although the Act orders schools to ensure that 100% of students test at levels identified as 'proficient' . . . the small per-pupil dollar allocation the law makes to schools serving low-income students is well under 10% of schools' total spending, far too little to correct these conditions (Darling-Hammond, 2007: 247–248). In short, the role of race and racism in perpetuating structural inequities was not considered in NCLB research.

Critical race theorists who rely on quantitative methods also accept the proviso that analyses cannot be separated from the analyst. In addition, as higher education scholars Van Dusen and Nissen (2020: 4) have recognized,

[a]ll data are socially constructed and reflect the hegemonic power structures that created them. Grades, for example, are social constructs created by instructors and codified by our educational systems. How instructors assign grades is an idiosyncratic process that reflects the values and beliefs of individual instructors and the power structures of their discipline and university, rather than an abstract truth about a student. In this sense, grades may represent a form of structural racism in the context of organizational or university practices that discriminate against marginalized persons. In effect, studies that rely on the quantitative measure of grades do not take into account racism, sexism, or classism, and therefore do not represent a "scientific truth" (Van Dusen and Nissen, 2020: 4).

Quantitative Studies

The caveats around the suitability of quantitative methods for CRT studies have perhaps created challenges for the use of quantitative CRMs across disciplines, particularly around measurement issues. Nonetheless, there are CRT studies that have relied on quantitative as well as mixed methods. For example, some CRT studies have considered the malleability of implicit racial bias, sometimes referred to as automatic racial bias, and the interventions that produce change (Neitzel, 2018). Social psychologists have manipulated social contexts that can moderate automatic racial bias favoring Whites, showing that bias can be partially or even completely attenuated under certain conditions (Barden et al., 2004; Dasgupta and Greenwald, 2001; Lowery, Hardin, and Sinclair, 2001). For instance, Wittenbrink, Judd, and Park (2001) ran two experiments to demonstrate the malleability of implicit bias toward Blacks.[9] They suggest that stereotypes and attitudes activated spontaneously from memory can be altered by situational or contextual cues. They varied their evaluative priming procedures by varying two visual contexts. In one study, White participants' implicit attitudes toward Blacks varied as a result of exposure to a positive (a family barbecue) or negative (a gang incident[10]) stereotypic situation. In another experiment, the visual contexts included a spray-painted wall (ostensibly, according to the researchers, indicative of a ghetto) and a church. In both instances, racial attitudes as measured by a sequential priming task where Whites viewed a positive stereotypic image helped to attenuate the racial biases of Whites.

---

[9] Online survey experiments help to measure racism implicitly when participants are provided with tasks or scenarios requiring them to respond to racial stimuli. One such tool is the evaluative priming task.

[10] This, in and of itself, suggests bias on the part of the researchers.

Van Dusen and Nissen (2020) rely on quantitative methods to investigate the relationship between the use of teaching assistants (TAs) and dropouts and withdrawal rates of Latinx from introductory physics courses. Admission into most STEM programs requires passing an introductory physics course. But physics courses have a disproportionately high failure rate among students who have and continue to be marginalized by racism, sexism, and classism. In effect, students of color are preempted or precluded from pursuing STEM degrees. Van Dusen and Nissen rely on data from 2,312 students in forty-one sections of introductory physics courses at a Hispanic Serving Institution in California. They developed hierarchical generalized linear models of student dropout rates that accounted for gender, race, first-generation status, and TA-supported instruction. They find strong support that the presence of TAs lowers dropout and withdrawal rates of male and female Latinx students. They conclude that reliance on TAs is "an appealing tool to improve equity on a large scale because [they] . . . create an interest convergence between marginalized students and those with power" (Van Dusen and Nissen, 2020: 11).

Huang, Apouey, and Andrews (2014) in their study examine the role of race and ethnicity in genetic-testing awareness. As they point out, there has been a proliferation of genetic information available through the Internet. Even genetic testing has become readily available online, which can help in the prevention and early detection of diseases and other health risks. They question whether there are race- and ethnicity-based disparities that result from lack of awareness, access, and utilization of online genetic information for testing as well as counseling. Their research relied on data from the National Cancer Institute's Health Information National Trends Survey (HINTS)[11] 2007 cross-sectional survey of a nationally representative sample of American adults: 7,674 American adults participated in the 2007 survey, which was conducted by telephone (using random digit dialing) and postal mail (using addresses from US Postal Service records). The survey asked questions about health services and knowledge of specific cancers, awareness of services, demographics, and the health background of participants. The research targeted online users only, which was perhaps a shortcoming, as Blacks and Latinx are less likely to use the Internet on smartphones, computers, tablets, or other devices than are Whites (Pew Research Center, 2019). The question pertaining to awareness of genetic testing asked: "Have you heard or read about any genetic tests?" The final sample included 3,432 respondents: Whites (2,911), Latinx (236), and Blacks

---

[11] HINTS is a cross-sectional survey of a nationally representative sample of American adults conducted biennially by the National Cancer Institute.

(285). Several independent variables were incorporated in the analysis to reflect demographic status, Internet use, health knowledge, and health attitudes.

Huang, Apouey, and Andrews' multivariate logistic regression analysis[12] found significant gaps between Whites and Blacks and Latinx around health-related knowledge, online information-seeking behaviors, and information trust of the Internet. The findings suggest that there is wide diversity by race in the amount of trust of online information sources and knowledge of the existence of online genetic testing.

Some critical race theorists have also called for the use of a mixed-methods approach. Covarrubias and colleagues (2018) applied a mixed-methods approach to studying the educational pipeline for Latinx students in order to promote a better understanding of the educational outcomes for racialized groups. They argued that an "overreliance on decontextualized quantitative data often leads to majoritarian interpretations. Without sociohistorical contexts, these interpretations run the risk of perpetuating culturally deficit ideologies about the causes that produce and reproduce these outcomes" (Covarrubias, et al., 2018: 253). Their qualitative data is obtained via "*testimonio*," or storytelling grounded in praxis, whereby the participant and the researcher coproduce the analysis of the story, which comports with CRT methods. California served as the case study. For quantitative data, they rely on the U.S. Census, which they argue are somewhat compromised as the categories employed are discrete and do not capture the nuances and complexities of intersectionality. First, demographic categories in the Census are fixed classifications; an example can be seen in gender that is categorized as either "male" or "female." It is thus challenging to link indicators of social class (e.g., wages) to gender and race/ethnicity categories, which are based on the data portraits selected by the Bureau and their understanding of which intersectional analyses matter.

Their quantitative findings show that of those Latinx who enroll in college in California, only around 17 percent will obtain some form of college degree, and around 15 percent will withdraw or drop out. The *testimonios*, however, add significant context to the quantitative findings. Covarrubias and colleagues discover that some of the following factors impact the educational pipeline for Latinx students:

---

[12] Multivariate logistic regression was used to examine the relationships between race and ethnicity and the dichotomous outcome (awareness of genetic testing) with and without adjusting for all variables related to sociodemographics, online information seeking behaviors, Internet use, and health knowledge. Huang, Apouey, and Andrews employed the nonlinear decomposition method to examine the extent to which there was an awareness gap among racial groups. This algorithm quantifies the contribution of each of the independent factors on racial differences and includes standard errors.

(1) When children of immigrants learn to speak English (e.g., before or after entering elementary school).

(2) Geographical location. For example, whether or not children had access to Catholic parochial education, which was deemed better than public schools in certain areas (e.g., East Los Angeles).

(3) Age of children; that is, oldest child often responsible for younger siblings and household maintenance when both parents working two jobs.

(5) Presence of grandparent(s) to offset responsibilities of oldest child.

There are many more factors that are too elaborate to document here, but the *testimonios* not only provide sociohistorical context to better describe the educational pipelines of Latinx children, but they are extraordinarily moving as well.

Gilbert and Ray (2016) provide some CRT prescriptions for improving quantitative studies that examine police behaviors that lead to what has been termed, "justifiable homicides" of Black men (also see Siegel, 2020). The recent deaths of several Black men at the hands of police (e.g., George Floyd, Philando Castile, Eric Garner, and Michael Brown) have revealed a pattern of criminalizing Black men; that is, where Blackness and criminality are viewed synonymously. This justifies to the police and perhaps society the excessive use of violence by police against Black men and women, which often results in the spurious rulings or findings of "justifiable homicides." This is certainly indicative of the recent killing of Breonna Taylor by three Louisville Metro police officers who fired their weapons during an aborted narcotics search that ended in Ms. Taylor's death. No homicide charges were filed against any of the three police officers.[13] The ruling by the grand jurors hinged on what Attorney General Daniel Cameron told reporters: Kentucky's "vigorous laws on self-defense," justify the homicide (Wolfson, 2020). Twenty-five states across the country have self-defense or "stand your ground" laws.[14]

Gilbert and Ray offer a number of suggestions for applying a quantitative CRT methodological framework to studies on police brutality and violence against Blacks in our society (see Table 1). As the table shows, some of the suggestions relate more to practice, yet these recommendations can certainly guide research as well, even in public administration and policy (e.g., where Gilbert and Ray mention training as it relates to race consciousness). Certainly, a CRT framework recognizes that most training programs, including implicit

---

[13] One of the officers was charged, not with Ms. Taylor's death, but with "wanton endangerment" for firing into a neighbor's apartment in Louisville.

[14] George Zimmerman was acquitted in the 2012 shooting death of Trayvon Martin on the claim that it was self-defense.

Table 1 Applying CRT to police brutality (context of "justifiable homicides").

Concept	Conventional definition	Conventional methodological approach	CRT methodological approach
Race consciousness	Deep awareness of one's racial position; awareness of racial stratification processes operating in colorblind contexts	Using crime statistics to "hot spot" police, who racially profile individuals and communities	Researchers, practitioners, policymakers, and police departments clarify their racial biases before collecting and analyzing data and develop strategies that are not based on negative racial perceptions. This includes training new police officers and other law enforcement agents and including research on racial prejudice in ongoing training.
Primacy of racialization	The fundamental contribution of racial stratification to societal problems; the central focus of CRT scholarship on explaining racial phenomena	Racial attributes become the dominant feature to develop policies and policing practices and dismiss systemic discrimination	Studies that understand the contexts and structures that lead to high crime in some communities and unequal life chances within those communities. Data collected from these studies should highlight differences by race

Race as a social construct	Significance that derives from social, political, and historical forces	Biological determinism – that posits race is meaningful because it provides insight about one's alleged biology and propensities, such as Black men are biologically predispositioned to commit crimes and their presence requires more severe control and force	...and gender as well as focus on social determinants that make those communities unhealthy. A study that assesses race not as a risk factor for crime, but identifies individuals of a racial/ethnic group, like Black men, who may be considered high risk for racial profiling and a specific group who has experienced racial profiling to unpack their experiences.
Gender as a social construct	Significance of gender constructions that derive from social, political, and historical forces	Being a biological male and understanding that manhood is an identity constructed through intrapersonal and interpersonal relationships	Understanding the factors that contribute to male identities, self-presentations, and performances within contexts such as families, schools, workplaces, public settings, and health-care settings that may increase levels of policing and enhance morbidity and mortality.

Table 1 (cont.)

Concept	Conventional definition	Conventional methodological approach	CRT methodological approach
"Ordinariness" of racism*	Racism is embedded in the social fabric of society	Racial exceptionalism that defines race as a set of rare, discrete, and overtly egregious incidents	A study on the mental and physical health impacts of everyday policing behaviors formally by police and informally by shop owners, restaurant owners, teachers, and health-care professionals.
Structural determinism	The fundamental role of macro-level forces in driving and sustaining inequities across time and contexts; the tendency of dominant group members and institutions to make decisions or take actions that preserve existing power hierarchies	Emphasizing individual or interpersonal factors (e.g., how Black males wear their clothes – hoodies, sagging pants; how they speak)	A multilevel study that considers how policy factors such as racial residential segregation and profiling laws promote and legalize policing. A study that empirically tests physiological, psychological, and behavioral responses to Black men in different scenarios, contexts, clothing, and speech use.
Social construction of knowledge	The claim that established knowledge within a discipline cannot be	The belief that empirical research is impermeable to social or political influences	A systematic review and meta-analysis of studies that criminalize Blacks and Black men positing that race is

	reevaluated using antiracism modes of analysis	(e.g., crimes are mostly committed by Black people, especially Black men)	a biological determinant [to show the spurious nature of research claiming race is biological and violence is innate].
Critical approaches	A social psychological approach to develop a comprehensive understanding of how individual biases develop prejudice and discrimination in social interaction	Accepting phenomena or explanations at face value	Researchers examine patterns and trends of crime by race, ethnicity, and gender and offer social psychological explanations about patterns of crime, racial profiling, and policing.
Intersectionality	The interlocking and multiplicative approach to co-occurring social categories (e.g., race and gender) and the social structures that maintain them	Additive models of separate and distinct social categories and identities (e.g., race, gender, sexual orientation, social class)	Efforts to address racial and gender stereotypes about Black men that negatively characterize them within a pathological framing, which may negatively impact their ability to obtain educational achievements, be legitimate participants in the labor market, access and use health-care services, and develop positive coping behaviors.

Table 1 (cont.)

Concept	Conventional definition	Conventional methodological approach	CRT methodological approach
Disciplinary self-critique	The systematic examination by members of a discipline of its conventions and impacts on the broader society	Limited critical examination of how a discipline's norms might influence the knowledge on a topic	Forging interdisciplinary research teams to work collaboratively and overcome the inability of disciplines to recognize "death by legal intervention" or "justified homicide" as a structural and institutional problem and to develop comprehensive solutions that address social and behavioral determinants.
Voice	Prioritizing the perspectives of marginalized persons; privileging the experiential knowledge of outsiders within	Routine privileging of majority voices, priorities, policies, and practices (e.g., Ferguson Police Department generating revenue from traffic and court fines and fees) that may lead to policing behaviors	Providing Black men who are at a high risk for being policed and have been policed informally and formally in multiple settings to discuss their experiences and to express potential solutions.

* The ordinariness of racism refers to the ubiquity of racism, not its absence, which characterizes society's normal state. Ordinariness challenges the erroneous, yet widely held belief that exposures to racism are perceptible because they are infrequent in an otherwise racism-free, society (Ford and Airhihenbuwa 2010).

Source: Adapted from, Keon L. Gilbert and Rashawn Ray. 2016. Why Police Kill Black Males with Impunity: Applying Public Health Critical Race Praxis (PHCRP) to Address the Determinants of Policing Behaviors and "Justifiable" Homicides in the USA. *Journal of Urban Health*, 93(Suppl 1): 122–140 at pp. 126–129.

bias training are often window dressing, unless they are institutionalized; that is, where training programs are offered regularly and on a long-term basis, rather than once-a-year, for only new workers or police recruits.

Finally, Gerido (2020: 39) provides a comprehensive review of quantitative studies examining racial health disparities, and offers ways in which a CRT framework could have strengthened the outcomes and interpretation of the research (see Appendix). She begins by pointing to racial disparities in breast cancer, for example, pointing out that Black women in the United States have the highest death rate from breast cancer despite having lower incidence rates when compared with White women. They are 39–44 percent more likely to die from breast cancer than White women. She notes that differential access to information and resources partly drive these health disparities; for example, genetic testing can offer Black women risk-reducing pharmacological or surgical treatment options. However, Black women have lower odds of being offered referrals to genetic counseling, their physicians are less likely to order genetic testing, and their concerns around historic injustices in medical research and genetics are ignored (Bliss, 2012; Hogarth, 2017; Jones, et al., 2017; Shields, et al., 2008). These challenges, she urges, must be considered in quantitative studies on racial disparities in mortality rates of women with breast cancer.

Gerido (2020) argues that one of the primary datasets to examine racial disparities in breast cancer is HINTS. But, as she points out, the HINTS instrument includes measures of race and ethnicity, but it does not include measures of racism or racial discrimination, which is a fundamental cause of health disparities and adverse health outcomes in racial and ethnic minorities (Williams et al., 2019). Thus, in one of the studies she reviewed – by Krakow and colleagues (2017), which involved the prevalence of genetic testing awareness by race and ethnicity – Gerido critiques the manner in which researchers conceptualized genetic testing awareness (also see Appendix). Gerido (2020: 49) points out that the Krakow study simply asked whether participants responded "yes" to the following question: "Doctors use DNA tests to analyze someone's DNA for health reasons. Have you heard or read about this type of genetic test?" Gerido argues that this question introduces bias because while many people may be aware of ancestry and paternity tests, they may not refer to them as genetic tests or they may not be aware that doctors use genetic tests for health reasons. Only those who answered "yes" to genetic testing awareness were also asked about the types of genetic tests they had ever received. In effect, the quantitatively analyzed data and the results were interpreted in ways which insufficiently represent Black women and their health information behaviors.

These and other studies demonstrate the viability of quantitative CRT studies, providing they account for racism, for example, and not simply race, as well as meeting the other stipulations described earlier. The following sections seek to address the potential utility of applying a CRT and CRMs to research in public administration.

Application of CRT to Public Administrative Studies

Many in the field of public administration have raised questions about not only how knowledge is produced, but also who produces it and how it is used (see, e.g., Raadschelders, 2011; Riccucci, 2010; Stivers, 2002; 2000; 1991). To be sure, different methods are appropriate for different aspects of social science research. Likewise, the theoretical lenses applied to public administrative studies vary based on their applicability. Following the tradition of other fields in the social sciences, the field of public administration would be advanced greatly by CRT and indeed it comports with the field's pursuit of social equity and justice (Riccucci, 2021). George Frederickson, one of the most prominent social equity scholars, referred to social equity as the "third" pillar of public administration. Writing for the New Public Administration[15] movement of the late 1960s, he argued that "[t]he rationale for Public Administration is almost always better (more efficient or economical) management. New Public Administration adds *social equity* to the classic objectives and rationale" (Frederickson, 1971: 311, emphasis in original). Frederickson thus advanced the seminal theoretical justifications for social equity as a critical value in public administration (Frederickson, 1974; 1980; 1990).

Susan Gooden (2014), also a renowned scholar of social equity, advanced an important justification for applying CRT to public administration. Gooden argued that the field of public administration has completely avoided discussions of race as a nervous area; in short, there is a fear and nervousness around even speaking about race issues. She states that "[o]ver the course of history, this nervousness has stifled many individuals and organizations, leading to an inability to seriously advance the reduction of racial inequities in government. Until this nervousness is effectively managed, public administration efforts to reduce inequities cannot realize their full potential" (Gooden, 2014: 3). She goes on to say that this nervousness "interferes significantly with the daily task of public agencies to provide governmental services in ways that align with our guiding democratic principles as set forth in the U.S. Constitution" (Gooden, 2014: 3). Indeed, a critical discourse analysis of racism and anti-Blackness in research in public administration indicates that scholars either reinforce or resist

---

[15] The New Public Administration grew out of the first Minnowbrook Conference in 1968. Dwight Waldo was one of the organizers of this conference that brought together a group of young scholars to address the social and political unrest of the 1960s.

addressing systemic, institutional racism (Trochmann, Viswanath, Puello and Larson, 2021). CRT encourages the field to overcome the fear and nervousness by explicitly confronting racism and racial inequality in order to not only advance the field, but to also combat the underlying structural racism in our political, social, and economic institutions. CRT maintains that research that ignores race may appear "neutral" but it adheres to and promotes the existing racial hierarchy whether intentional or unintentional.

And, as noted earlier, critical theories[16] in a broad sense have been applied to public administrative phenomena.[17] For example, Camila Stivers is a pioneer in the effort to study public administration from a feminist perspective that can provide insights into the application of CRT to public administrative research (also see Hutchinson, 2002; 2001; Hutchinson and Mann, 2006; 2004; Shields, 2006; 2005).[18] First, Stivers (1991: 64) makes this essential clarification about theory: "By 'theory,' of course, I mean something much closer to political philosophy than what is arrived at by linking empirically tested hypotheses. I view public administration as a form of governance. As such, its most interesting questions are inherently value-laden and must therefore be dealt with by means of reasoned argument rather than proof." This echoes what various critical theorists, discussed earlier in the context of CRT, have called for: ontological, epistemological, and axiological shifts in how knowledge and reality are constructed. That is, if research seeks to rely on quantitative methodologies in feminist study, then "gendered logic," "gendered statistics," and gender as a social construct must be accounted for, as well as acknowledging that data are not neutral and researchers cannot be completely objective.

Stivers (1991: 50) goes on to say that "feminist theory is critical of existing reality. Feminists view women's historical exclusion from certain human pursuits (such as politics)

---

[16] There are varieties of critical theory including, for example, postcolonial criticism, focusing on the hegemonistic powers of colonists, and the Frankfurt School perspective, which applies Marxism to a radical interdisciplinary social theory (see, Sementelli and Abel, 2000; Wiggershaus, 1994). The Frankfurt School grew out of the frustration and dissatisfaction of intellectuals, academics, and political dissidents with the contemporary socioeconomic systems (capitalist, fascist, communist) of the 1930s.

[17] Queer theory has also been applied in public administration, including in the context of LGBTQIA+ issues (see, for example, Lee, Learmonth and Harding, 2008; Matthews and Poyner, 2020; Taylor, 2007).

[18] It should be noted, however, that many feminist scholars distinguish between feminist theory and critical theory (see, Campbell and Bunting, 1991; Hesse-Biber, 2014). As Martin (2003: 66), for example, points out "Some feminists are liberal advocates of equal opportunity, while others endorse more radical alternatives. In other words, there are both critical and non-critical versions of feminist scholarship." She further argues that feminist theorists place gender and sex at the core of their analyses, whereby critical theorists focus primarily on class.

and confinement to others (such as homemaking) as, if not always deliberate on the part of individual men, certainly not 'natural.' Feminists argue that such arrangements make women more likely than men to encounter neglected perspectives and to ask submerged questions about the terms and characteristics of our common existence." Gender is the fundamental element in social analyses of women's role in public administrative affairs and examining the existing philosophy of public administration through a gender lens can help reshape the field's understanding of women's role in such substantive areas as administrative knowledge, the politics-administration dichotomy, the nature of administrative discretion, and the dimensions of the administrative state (also see D'Agostino and Levine, 2011).

In her celebrated book, *Gender Images in Public Administration*, Stivers (2002) challenges the field's obsession with such ideas as objectivity and neutral competence, arguing that objectivity and neutrality especially with regards to "science" relies on a set of norms that conform to men's conception of the world. Competence has been defined in terms of the heroic and virtuous male professional who sacrifices his personal and family life for his career, where women, consequently, are relegated to an inferior, menial existence. Stivers (2002: 45) also observes that

> the state has never been neutral on the subject of women – in fact, at the time when Wilson and Goodnow were urging administrative neutrality, women still could not vote. If Wilson, who was teaching at Bryn Mawr College when he penned his famous essay in 1887, had listened to his students (all females) on the issue of suffrage instead of disdaining and patronizing them, he might have been more cautious about concluding that "the weightier debates of constitutional principle" were "no longer of more immediate practical moment than questions of administration"
> (quoting Wilson 1887: 200).

These male founders of the field formulated a philosophy or "principles" of public administration when women were legitimately viewed and treated as unequal to men, and were fulfilling the "God-given role" of wife, mother, domestic and purveyor of moral purity.[19]

Janet Hutchinson and Patricia Shields, also pioneers in applying a feminist lens to their studies in public administration, have similarly pushed the

---

[19] Also see Stivers' 2000 treatise, *Bureau Men, Settlement Women*, where she takes a feminist perspective of women's early contributions to the public administration as settlement workers, which has largely been ignored. Women helped to establish and run settlement houses, where they worked to improve the lives of the urban poor and European immigrants, and to ultimately get governments to adopt settlement houses. Stivers' book helps to reconceive and reevaluate the intellectual history of public administration by showing the role of women in the development of the administrative state.

boundaries of the field to consider the importance of women in its history.[20] Indeed, Hutchinson (2002) points to the significance of women in our democracy, arguing that "deep democracy" and other models of participatory government will fail unless women enjoy full and equal participation in our governing institutions. As she argues, "en-gendered democracy is a multigendered democracy. Multigendering is based on the notion that gender is not static, is relational, fluid, and changing in reference to the environment. The relational aspects of gendering, once understood and accepted, may be an answer to the dilemma of the representation of women and our equal participation in the institutions that govern our lives" (Hutchinson, 2002: 721). In addition, Hutchinson and Mann (2004) raise the important concern that other disciplines are "fluent" in feminism but public administration is not. They argue that instead of calling out public administration to account for its insensitivity to basic gender inequities, the approach should be to "desensitize through knowledge production the language of feminisms, with the open goal of bringing truth to power" (Hutchinson and Mann, 2004: 86).[21]

Hutchinson and Mann, for example, question representative bureaucracy and organizational socialization theories as presuming that bureaucratic organizations are neutral, non-gendered structures. But they further argue that women in the bureaucracy will push for their counterparts in society only when they achieve a critical mass within the bureaucracy. In this context, they say "A vision comes to mind: women huddling together in the face of hegemonic masculinity, expressing their views only when their number reaches some critical mass, and making like the guys when it doesn't" (Hutchinson and Mann, 2004: 87). They go on to say that only a revolution would replace the hegemonic masculine organizational paradigm with one steeped in a feminist ideal, but they recognize that this is an unlikely scenario. They instead propose a multicultural, multigendered administration "that challenges the restrictive constructs that define us and determine our relationships to one another and to the organizations in which we work .... [they] suggest that this new paradigm, grounded in postmodern feminist and queer theories, problematizes extant PA methods and encourages engagement in an introspective evaluation of our own cultural and gendered boundaries. It also suggests ways in which we might cross those boundaries and enter entirely new worlds" (Hutchinson and Mann, 2004: 79).

---

[20] See the works of Shields (2006; 2005) and Shields and Soeters (2017), which applies classical and feminist pragmatism to her studies of Jane Addams, a forerunner of the settlement house movement, who was generally overlook in the intellectual history of public administration.

[21] There is no single type of feminism. Feminisms refers to the various types of feminism including liberal, radical, Marxist, and socialist to name a few.

The works of these prominent scholars point to the importance of going beyond "traditional" theory to investigate public administrative phenomena.[22] And as with critical race theorists, these trailblazers reject the prevailing orthodoxy that scholarship would or could be bias free, and that gender, as a social construct, could be consistently conceptualized or measured across studies. Moreover, like CRT, feminist theory places attention on institutional and structural inequalities, social and economic, between women and men, and offers ways to promote change. A qualitative approach seems to be the norm in feminist theory as applied to public administration.

The Qualitative Case

A pioneering qualitative study applying a CRT framework can be seen in Brandi Blessett's study of the implementation of one of the first urban renewal rehabilitation projects in Baltimore, Maryland. Blessett (2020) begins by pointing out that the racial tensions permeating much of the twentieth century greatly limited efforts to promote racial justice in any systemic or structural manner. She argues that "for politicians, the business elite, and the broader White public, racial justice was not deemed a priority when implementing urban renewal programs. In fact, urban blight and abandonment was approached with a race-neutral lens that focused on quantitative measures like effectiveness, efficiency, and economy. Fairness, justice, and equity were not considerations for Black residents in Baltimore, who were often characterized as being contributors to blight, abandonment, and dysfunction of cities, rather than victims of institutional racism and discriminatory practices" (Blessett 2020, 838). In Baltimore and in other parts of the country, urban renewal, which is aimed at revitalizing the economic viability of inner cities in particular, became more synonymous with gentrification, or as Blessett astutely puts it "Negro removal."

In her study, Blessett illustrates how the tools of government, including economic, institutional, personnel, and linguistic contextualize how administrative decisions resulted in racially disproportionate outcomes for Blacks in the Harlem Park neighborhood of Baltimore. For example, she examines of the sociohistorical patterns of racist actions by the city of Baltimore including segregating Blacks into neighborhoods that would ultimately lead to substandard education and housing (read: slums). Legal tools, such as the Housing Act of 1949 sought to clear slums and redevelop communities. But as noted earlier in this text, racism is embedded in laws, policies, and institutions that ultimately uphold and reproduce racial inequalities. Blessett also illustrates how Baltimore

---

[22] See Naylor, Wyatt-Nichol and Brown (2015) who suggests using CRT to examine the achievement gap and school dropout rates for Black males because institutional racism may be the cause.

relied on eminent domain – where the city appropriated desirable properties throughout Black neighborhoods and then transferred them to private entities for the purpose of redevelopment – without improving housing conditions for Blacks. In addition, because the Housing Act allowed federal funds to be funneled to local governments directly, cities such as Baltimore were able to manipulate the use of those funds for other purposes besides housing for Blacks.

Over time, several million dollars were invested in efforts to rehabilitate the economic and physical infrastructure of Baltimore; but the outcome had a disproportionately adverse impact of Blacks. Blessett (2020, 847) shows that as a result, "more than 25,000 people were displaced by urban renewal, public housing, and school construction from 1950 to 1964 – 90% of those relocated were Black residents . . . The outcome created two cities: one affluent, White, and business oriented and the other poor, Black, and disenfranchised. Despite all the quantitative good that was occurring in the city (e.g., overall numbers of acres set for redevelopment, the building roads and homes, refurbishing historic areas), the quality of life (e.g., the racial and social tension) for Black residents continued to worsen." Blessett offers a number of other examples to show how local government administrators' behaviors and actions perpetuated structural and institutional racism in Baltimore, ironically as it sought to improve the quality of life for its Black residents.

In addition, and similar to Stivers' reliance on a feminist perspective to examine the administrative state, Alexander and Stivers (2020; 2010) apply a critical lens to examine how historical understandings of the administrative state have neglected the influence of racial bias on the development of administrative practices (also see Alexander, 1997; Portillo, Bearfield and Humphrey, 2020; Witt, 2006). One might argue that this is a qualitative CRT study, as it follows all the tenets discussed about. They point out that "[a]dministration is not, in fact, a matter of disconnected neutrality, but is shaped and guided by historical narratives, among other factors in its environment. Narratives impart meaning, but they also limit positive change and promote 'institutional monoculturalism' afflicted with unexamined prejudice" (Alexander and Stivers, 2020: 1471). They argue that there are a number of significant, yet ignored factors that impact administrative practices and structures. The historical, disparaging treatment of persons of color, for example, has been ignored as well as the impact of racial biases that have been written into US law and public policy. Alexander and Stivers also point to administrative interpretations of public policy that facilitate and perpetuate racism. They provide an incisive descriptive and narrative account of these practices, including, for example, the treatment of Blacks by one of the field's founders, President Woodrow Wilson. When he became president, and learned that Blacks were employed in the federal service in a variety of managerial and supervisory capacities, he promptly reinstituted segregation in the federal government workforce. Black men with law degrees were moved to positions that Wilson viewed were more fitting: clerical and custodial jobs. President Wilson also embraced the Ku Klux Klan thus erasing any gains made by Blacks since Reconstruction. Overt racism was now rampant in the federal service and beyond, depriving Blacks the opportunities to participate in the running of the administrative state.

Alexander and Stivers also point to overtly racist laws such as the federal Naturalization Acts of 1790, 1795, 1798, and 1802 (defining citizens as free White persons) and the Asian Immigration Act of 1875 (excluding Asians) and other historical events steeped in racism to conclude that public administration and the administrative state were far from neutral and scientific. They go on to say that "[i]f administrative practice is to become less shaped by racial bias, the challenge for public administrators starts with becoming conscious of the myriad ways racism has, since the creation of the United States, infected laws and policies so that what look like neutral banisters to guide administrative decision-making are anything but. They must also confront how racism has, even more insidiously, hidden itself within administrative precedent that have guided their decisions" (Alexander and Stivers, 2020: 1486).

Witt (2006) has also examined how race has shaped scholarly output in public administration and that race and administrative study and practice in America have been intertwined since the inception of the field (also see Bearfield, 2009; Portillo and Humphrey, 2018). At the center of his CRT qualitative, legal analysis is the 1896 US Supreme Court decision, *Plessy* v. *Ferguson*, which legally established the "separate but equal" legislative and administrative doctrine. The intellectual construction of race that drew from that decision overshadowed the field. A "profoundly race-obsessed historiography" emanated from that decision and a "race preoccupation was especially evident in American political science journals between 1880 and 1910 . . . [and] the social and intellectual construction of race thus shadowed public administration at its founding" (Witt, 2006: 37). In effect, race, as Witt goes on to say, deeply shaped the theory and practice of public administration. He further argues that no journal articles nor books related to the field of public administration (e.g., *Political Science Quarterly*) directly attacked the separate but equal doctrine of *Plessy*, which "gave credence to and justification for white racial supremacy" in the field (Witt, 2006: 38).

Lutton (2010) has pointed out that critical theory has been used in qualitative research in public administration, especially by those who advocate for positive change. This is certainly a normative view, which speaks volumes to the normative basis of public administration, especially socially aware public administration. This suggests that knowledge is inevitably normative and political. Lutton (2010: 14) argues that "[m]any public administrators are interested in initiating change in social systems and collective institutions," and they have taken a critical approach to studying public administrative phenomenon. He further states that public administration is enhanced by qualitative critical approaches, including thick description that can address causation. Lutton writes (2010: 11), "[u]nlike quantitative research, qualitative research allows causal explanations to be understood as ideographic and emergent, as an unfolding of interconnected actions."

CRT is important in qualitative studies because it shows recognition and acceptance of tacit knowledge. As Lutton (2010: 12) suggests, "[t]here are some kinds of knowledge that are difficult (perhaps impossible) to observe directly. Still, there is indirect evidence supporting that knowledge. Qualitative research approaches provide a valuable way of recognizing, understanding, and sharing such tacit forms of knowledge." Certainly, racism, which is difficult to measure directly, as discussed earlier, is one such area that could be addressed qualitatively within CRT. Lutton also points to other criteria of CRT addressed earlier, including the lack of neutrality and objectivity and the social construction of reality.

Critical theory in public administration tends to rely on qualitative analysis. However, a more explicit reliance on CRT to study issues of race and racism could benefit the field immensely, especially through narratives, storytelling, and ethnographies. For example, Bearfield (2020) recently wrote about The BLM movement and its impact on the relationship between Black families and law enforcement. He spoke about "The Talk," "the conversation Black families have with their teenage children, most often their sons, on how to deal with police officers. Like families of all races, Black children are taught to address the police with respect. However, what makes the talk different, is the belief that the lessons learned during this conversation can mean the difference between life and death. Like many Black males, I can remember the moment I had the talk with my father. The way he taught me to talk, move, and behave when stopped by a police officer" (Bearfield, 2020: 3). He goes on to say that "[w]e rarely hear from Black police officers when we discuss police reform" (ibid). Narratives or stories that draw explicitly on such experiences illuminate not only how Blacks are taught to behave in the presence of police officers, but it exemplifies the privileges Whites enjoy in society. Whites need not keep their hands at "10 and 2" or "9 and 3" on an automobile's steering wheel, or be polite about being stopped for traveling five miles per hour over the speed limit. We can and do question police officer behavior when we are pulled over as a protection of our First Amendment rights, without fearing retaliation or violence for doing so.

Bearfield points to the importance of talking to Black police officers in our efforts to help study and bring about police reform. He argues, "[u]nlike most of my friends, I had the talk with my Dad, the police officer. We rarely hear from Black police officers when we discuss police reform. Like my father, they have an intimate knowledge of both the dangers of the job and the fear that many of their White colleagues have of young Black teens. If we are going to get serious about reforming our institutions, we must find a way to center the voice of Black police officers. Any hope of transformation will hinge on our ability to hear, and act on, their unique perspective" (Bearfield, 2020: 3).

Police reform, then, is one example where CRT can be applied to public administration scholarship with qualitative methods. Police violence against Blacks is central to public administration and management as police officers are street-level bureaucrats whose purpose is to protect the public. Policing is a public service, yet the service disproportionally favors and serves Whites. The BLM movement, which emerged in response to the acquittal of George Zimmerman in the shooting death of the Black teenager, Trayvon Martin, has led to a number of protest around the police killings of George Floyd, Breonna Taylor, Michael Brown, Erik Salgado, Eric Garner, Andrés Guardado, Atatiana Jefferson, Stephon Clark, Philando Castille, Alton Sterling, Freddie Gray, Sean Monterrosa, and a number of other Black and Latinx persons.

Police violence against Black and Brown persons raises questions around accountability and transparency, but the racism that underlies the violent behaviors of police is what requires examination (see, e.g., Headley and Wright, 2020 and Wright and Headley, 2020). Although they did not rely explicitly on CRT, Wright and Headley's (2021) qualitative study addresses the perception and use of body-worn cameras (BWCs) by police to determine if this technology promotes the accountability of police and whether it builds trust between the citizenry and the police. They point to the growth in use of BWCs across the United States, where seventy-five large cities have equipped their police officers with BWCs since 2012. Much of the research, they state, has focused on police officers' behaviors, including the use of force, arrests, and stop-and-frisk. Their study of a police district in Washington, D.C. included a qualitative analysis of forty semi-structured interviews of persons who attended Advisory Neighborhood Commissioners (ANCs) meetings – twenty-six of the interviewees were Black, and fourteen were White. The ANCs are neighborhood organizations comprised of locally elected representatives to help build closer ties between the local government and its citizens.

Wright and Headley were particularly interested in whether the use of BWCs would increase citizens' perceptions of police officer legitimacy as well as their accountability and approachability. Their findings revealed that most citizens consistently believed that BWCs may improve transparency, accountability, and police officer behavior. However, their results were less clear around whether citizens were more willing to approach a police officer with a BWC compared to one without a BWC. They found that twenty of the forty interviewed stated that they would never approach an officer, with or without a BWC. Those twenty were all Black. Wright and Headley (2021: 21) reported some of the citizens' comments here, including, "Approach them for what?"; "Why would I approach an officer?" and "There is a 50/50 chance that I would EVER APPROACH AN OFFICER" (emphasis in original). These reactions certainly help our understanding of citizens' resistance to approach an officer. Indeed, as Wright and Headley (2021: 19) point out, "qualitative research methods... are able to delve deeper into the perceptions of citizens" and "can further interrogate how citizens view the use and implementation of BWC to fully understand its influence on an array of intended policy outcomes."

Wright and Headley (2021: 23) conclude that

> [w]hile this study did not explicitly explore how different racial and ethnic groups view police officers, the interviews revealed a stark divide about which group feels more comfortable approaching a police officer – with Blacks indicating more negative sentiments. It may not necessarily be a surprising finding, given the current and historical climate regarding police–community relations with Black communities and other groups of color. However, the persistence of this finding in spite of new technological adoptions (i.e., BWC) designed to improve police–community relations is indeed telling. There needs to be a concerted effort by police departments to understand the limits of BWC being used to build bridges between the Black community and the police. Citizens across the country have witnessed more Black Americans killed by police, which fragments the relationship between the two parties. Having the Black community involved and more engaged in the implementation of BWC can be used as a participatory democracy tool in efforts to improve police–community relations.

Studies of police behaviors and violence from a CRT perspective would go even further. They could ask, for example: Are White police fearful of potential force or resistance from Blacks? Do they resent being questioned by Blacks? Police often become violent particularly when Blacks engage in constitutionally protected free speech. Eric Garner, for example, was stopped by police in 2014 for selling "loosies" (i.e., individual cigarettes) on a New York city street corner. When he stated that he was tired of being harassed by the police, officers attempted to restrain him by putting him in an illegal choke hold. Despite pleas from Garner that "I can't breathe," additional officers moved in to restrain him. He died in part as a result of the choke hold.

Or do White police fear Black men for other reasons? Some research suggests that White supremacy intersects with Black masculinity, slavery, and racism (see, e.g., Ferber, 2007). Orelus (2010) discusses the historical legacy of slavery in terms of the continued patterns of oppression against Black men. He states that

> if one wants to understand contemporary versions of black masculinity, one has to understand that after slavery there was a continuation of the violence exercised against black men in the labor market, in the streets, etc. Therefore, black men have to preform two jobs: (1) to be obedient in public interactions with whites or else suffer from indignities and potential death and (2) as a response to this, to be hyper masculine at home (Orelus, 2010: 63).

Others have pointed to the issue of "manhood," which is more than a metaphor for personhood and equality; it suggests Black men, unlike White men, are less than men (see, Jones, 1998). James Baldwin (1961: 28–29) wrote in the context of manhood that

> there was something which all black men held in common, something which cuts across opposing points of view, and placed in the same context of their widely dissimilar experience ....What ... black men held in common was their ache to come into the world as men.[23]

These issues and concerns lend themselves to CRMs that are qualitative – counter-narratives, ethnographies, hermeneutics, grounded theory, and case studies – which can root out the racist behaviors that trigger police violence and contextualize it more accurately as compared to CRMs that are quantitative.[24] And, importantly, Black police officers' associations across the country, marginalized by police departments and the official unions representing police officers, have been calling for police reform in response to the violence against Blacks in our society.[25] Black police officers and their representatives are working to change the culture of policing, which has been opposed by leaders of powerful official police unions, including local chapters

---

[23] Another interpretation relates to the phallus. As Jones (1998: 47) points out, the bodies of Black men are "equated with a penis." This, too, may pose a threat to White men/police, thus inciting violence against Black men.

[24] Greenberg (2014) has suggested that quantitative analyses of police practices such as stop-and-frisk are ineffective. His study ultimately found that, contrary to police departments' policies, stop-and-frisk resulted in no evidence that misdemeanor arrests led to a reduction in such crimes as homicide, robbery, or aggravated assaults.

[25] Grand Council of Guardians, a Black law enforcement association in New York, and the Miami Community Police Benevolent Association, Miami's largest Black police association, are among these Black police officers' associations.

of Police Benevolent Unions and Fraternal Orders of Police. Their stories and narratives would contribute greatly to a body of knowledge in public administration that is aimed at police reform.[26]

Studying how racism persists and continues to promote inequalities in our field is another area where CRT can be applied. Portillo (2020: 4), for example, points out that while the field works "to meaningfully incorporate Black Indigenous and People of Color perspectives into the top scholarship and practice in public management, we must recognize the overt and covert ways the voices of BIPOC scholars are marginalized and the implication the myth of neutrality has had on practice in communities across our globe." She goes on to say that "[s]tudying inequality, or racialized differences in outcomes, without understanding the policies and practices that created the context for inequalities to thrive is no longer enough. We have plenty of empirical evidence of inequalities, but we lack rich theoretical discussions around how racism has and continues to perpetuate inequalities" (ibid). Portillo urges the field to think more critically about these issues, which certainly includes the application of CRT through narratives, counter-stories and counternarratives (also see Merritt, 2020; Wright and Merritt, 2020).

In this vein, applying CRT to qualitative studies in public administration includes investigating employment discrimination and microaggressions at the microlevel. For example, Blacks and Latinx experiencing the effects of discriminatory hiring practices in the public sector represents a hallmark case of how institutional racism manifests in public organizations. Exploring the narratives of case law is indicative of the actual experiences of Black and Brown people who have been discriminated against. Interviewing some of the individuals behind these lawsuits can provide a richer context for their experiences of discrimination based on race or ethnicity and the lasting effects it has produced. What policies and behaviors exactly led to the discriminatory practices? Did the organizational culture enable or facilitate the discriminatory treatment? Was there evidence of systemic or structural forms of racism (i.e., public policies, institutional practices, cultural representations, and other norms that reinforce and perpetuate racial group inequity)? The individual stories they tell can elucidate the broader trends of employment discrimination as well as the

---

[26] Also see McGregor's (2016) qualitative study on the political feasibility of instituting a civilian review board to address police violence in the city of Newark. She conducted interviews with current or retired police officers as well as elected officials and representatives of grassroots advocacy organizations that had pushed for a review board. She found that a federal investigation into police practices in Newark combined with grassroots support and the election of an activist mayor, Ras Baraka, son of the poet and activist Amiri Baraka, resulted in the creation of the city's first police civilian review board. Also see mixed-methods CRT studies by Torres, Driscoll and Burrow (2010) and Heynen, Perkins and Roy (2006), discussed later in this text.

complexities of workplace inequality. The litigants' insights could also assist in promoting remedies for the pernicious, enduring problem of discrimination based on race and ethnicity, or even discrimination at the intersection of race, ethnic, and gender.

Even beyond case law, interviewing a sample of say, Black and Latinx academics in political science or public administration, would be particularly revealing. Because racism is institutionalized, it is almost certain that Black and Latinx scholars have faced discriminatory practices in their career. Counter-stories here would lead to insights on racial characterizations and stereotypes and help contextualize the everyday experiences and the social processes that result in racism. They can also reveal the institutional behaviors that led to inequities in the workplace and potential ways to combat them. Similarly, marginalized groups commonly face microaggressions; these are the everyday slights, insults, and derogatory remarks that were not necessarily intended to cause harm, but they actually do to the recipient of those remarks. An example can be found in a White person stating to a Black person: "I could never be racist because I have Black friends." Or, when a White woman clutches her purse when a Black person approaches (Sue, 2010). The cumulative effect of micro-aggressions includes adverse physical and emotional health, including depression, anxiety, fatigue, anger, chronic infections, thyroid problems, and high blood pressure.

Rengifo and Pater (2017) examine, with qualitative methods, microaggressions by police against Black and Latinx youth. A good deal of research finds that police practices and behaviors are not racially neutral; Blacks and Latinx are more likely to be stopped by police compared to whites (Brunson, 2007; Harris, 2002; Tyler and Wakslak, 2004). Based on interviews with forty-three Black and Latinx youth in New York City, Rengifo and Pater find that structural racism is embedded in the microaggressions against Black and Latinx youth in their encounters with police. The youth reported that police held unwarranted suspicions about them as criminals simply because of their race or ethnicity, and that the police treated them as inferior, also because of their ethnicity or race. Respondents reported being stopped by police in plain clothes and searched without reason or probable cause. When asked for IDs from the police, the officers often flashed their guns. In some cases, respondents stated that inter-actions with Black police officers were much more congenial than with White police (Rengifo and Pater, 2017).[27]

---

[27] For additional qualitative studies relying on CRT to examine microaggressions (racism at the microlevel), which could be studied in public administration, see for example, Solórzano, Ceja and Yosso, 2000; Williams, et.al., 2020.

In sum, there are an abundance of opportunities to apply CRT to qualitative research in public administration.[28] While virtually no quantitative studies in the field rely explicitly on CRT, the following section provides some examples of where it would be appropriate.

The Quantitative Case

Quantitative research in public administration must certainly accept the criteria set forth by critical race theorists discussed earlier, regarding, for example, acknowledgment that research cannot be value-free, neutral, or purely objective, that race is a social construct and concomitantly that measuring race or racism directly is nearly impossible. And CRMs that are quantitative must recognize the existence of white normativity, whereby whiteness is viewed as "natural and right" and the norm. As critical race theorists maintain, whiteness informs research as well as practice (see, Bearfield, Humphrey and Portillo, 2021).

While some may argue that quantitative CRMs are simply not suitable for studying public administrative phenomena, particularly because of the normative foundation of the field, certain topics may lend themselves to quantitative analysis. One example is in the area of environmental justice, which is the fair treatment of all people regardless of race, color, national origin, or income with respect to the development, implementation and enforcement of environmental laws, regulations and policies.[29] A plethora of studies have demonstrated that Blacks, ethnic minorities, indigenous persons and other people of color, as well as low-income communities are disproportionately affected adversely by environmental exposure from air, water, and soil pollution that emanates from consumer practices, industrialization, and militarization (Mohai, Pellow and Roberts, 2009).

We may recall the Flint, Michigan water disaster, for example, that began in 2014 and lasted through 2019, where the drinking water was contaminated with lead and Legionnaires' disease, due to Flint's decision to change its water source from treated Detroit Water and Sewerage Department to the Flint River. Close to 60 percent of Flint is comprised of Blacks, who were hit hardest by this disaster. Because corrosion inhibitors were not applied to the water, lead from aging pipes seeped into the water supply, leading to, and exposing city residents to extremely elevated levels of lead. Thousands of people suffered

---

[28] Additional research that can assist in applying CRT to qualitative studies in public administration include, for example, Parker (1998, affirmative action); Dickinson (2012, environmental justice); Kurtz (2009, environmental justice); Lynn and Parker (2006, urban education/schooling); Smith-Maddox and Solórzano (2002, teaching in diverse classrooms) and Parker, Deyhle, and Villenas (2019, administrative policy).

[29] For qualitative CRT studies on environmental justice see, for example, Richter, 2018 and Pulido, 2000.

lead poisoning and at least twelve people died after more than eighty people were infected with Legionnaires' disease. The Michigan Department of Environmental Quality responded very slowly to the tragic water crisis, and it was later determined by the Mayor's office, that race and class were factors in the authorities' slow and dishonest response to Flint's water crisis (Benz, 2019; Pauli, 2019; Pulido, 2016).

Environmental justice can be studied via quantitative CRMs, because it is the underlying racism that leads to inequalities and inequities in the government's delivery of clean air and water, and overall safe environmental conditions. Historical, systemic and structural racism, and implicit bias have led to environmental disasters that disproportionately affect communities of color; and climate change further exacerbates economic inequalities. Polluted water and air are racial justice matters; this has even been recognized recently by environmental justice activists following the police killing of George Floyd: they have been intoning, "I can't breathe" (Chow, 2020).

Heynen, Perkins and Roy's (2006) mixed-methods study of environmental justice is a good example here.[30] Their research shows how urban trees can affect quality of life. They say that "the spatially inequitable distribution of urban trees in relation to race and ethnicity is yet another instance of urban environmental inequality" (Heynen, Perkins and Roy, 2006: 3). Their study, which integrates urban-tree canopy cover[31] data from aerial photography, U.S. Census data, and qualitative data collected through in-depth interviews, finds that there is an inequitable distribution of urban canopy cover within Milwaukee, Wisconsin, which disadvantages and adversely affects the quality of life for Blacks and Latinx in their inner-city communities. Neighborhoods across the country with a majority Blacks and Latinx tend to have a higher share of concrete surfaces and an extremely limited number of tress and parks with canopy cover. Although Heynen, Perkins, and Roy do not explicitly develop measures for racism, their data on urban-tree canopy cover illustrates along with race, ethnicity, and household income variables that Milwaukee's non-Hispanic White populations are correlated more with canopy cover as compared with the city's predominantly inner-city, communities of color. Trees trap air pollutants and improve mental and physical health; in particular, they help to reduce incidences of acute respiratory symptoms (Nowak, et.al., 2014). As Leahy and Serkez (2021: online) point out, "The red

---

[30] Holifield (2009: 638) writes that critical studies of environmental justice have largely been absent from the environmental justice field. His work, although qualitative, can provide some guidance to CRT quantitative studies in public administration and policy.

[31] Urban-tree canopy cover refers to the layer of tree leaves, branches, and stems that provide tree coverage. It makes urban communities more sustainable and livable, by, for example, reducing summer peak temperatures and air pollution and improving social ties among neighbors. It can also enhance property values and provide aesthetic benefits for urban communities.

lines that were drawn around neighborhoods – predominantly Black as well as Catholic, Jewish and immigrant – now often line up very closely with maps showing a lack of tree canopy today."

Mohai, Pellow and Roberts (2009) suggest that environmental justice can also be referred to as environmental racism.[32] They provide a comprehensive review of studies relying on efforts to quantitatively measure environmental injustice or racism (e.g., zip codes, census tracts, or concentric circles) and conclude first, that CRT studies should be included in research on environmental justice and that current measures of injustice or racism (e.g., zip codes) need to be refined and expanded.[33]

Indeed, most CRT quantitative studies tend to rely on self-reported discrimination,[34] which is generally accepted as the best approach for measuring individual-level racism (Krieger, 2012). However, work by some scholars has helped to advance frameworks and generate new methods for understanding and measuring racism at the structural level in our society (see, e.g., Chambers, et. al., 2018; Groos, et. al., 2018; Jones, 2002; Krieger, 1999; 2012; Williams and Mohammed, 2013). Table 2 provides examples of a number of studies that seek to measure structural-level racism. These measures, discussed further shortly, can be applied to public administration and policy research in areas such as employment, health care, policing – and police brutality as addressed earlier – political participation, and immigration.

A study by Chambers and colleagues (2018) is perhaps one of the most informative CRT studies that relies on quantitative methods. Their research falls in the area of public health, which is relevant for public administration and policy. They examine the association between structural racism and birth outcomes among Black and White women. Black women are two to three times more likely to have an infant born at low birth weight or premature compared to White women. They offer "traditional" and "novel" measures for structural or institutional racism, and their findings indicate that traditional

---

[32] Benjamin Chavis, then executive director of the Commission for Racial Justice of the United Church of Christ, coined the term environmental racism in 1982 and defined it as "racial discrimination in environmental policy making, the enforcement of regulations and laws, the deliberate targeting of communities of color for toxic waste facilities, the official sanctioning of the life-threatening presence of poisons and pollutants in our communities, and the history of excluding people of color from leadership of the ecology movements" (Mohai, Pellow and Roberts, 2009: 406–407).

[33] For other useful empirically quantitative studies applying CRT to environmental justice see, for example, Heynen (2003) and Hamilton (1995). Also see meta-analyses by Ringquist (2005) and Mohai & Bryant (1992) on race and class disparities in the distribution of environmental hazards, which found environmental disparities were based on race.

[34] Asking explicit questions about racial discrimination, microaggression, and unfair treatment, and if it was reported. See, for example, Basford, Offermann and Behrend's (2014) study of microaggressions against women.

Table 2 Measuring inequity: description of included studies

Author(s)	Domain(s)	Racial ethnic comparisons	Measure(s) of structural racism[*]
Albert et al., 2010	Perceived racism in social institutions	Black-White	Summary score of responses to three questions: if respondent ever treated unfairly (1) on the job (hiring, promotion, and firing); (2) in housing (renting, buying, and mortgage); and (3) by the police (stopped, searched, and threatened) because of their race.
Chambers et al., 2017	Political participation, criminal justice, residential segregation	Black-White	Compared traditional measures to novel measures of structural racism. Traditional: Dissimilarity index, delta index, isolation index. Novel: Felony incarcerations, Racial composition of county board of supervisors.
Gee, 2008	Residential neighborhood/ housing	Chinese Americans- White	Redlining index of mortgage discrimination.
Greer et al., 2014	Perceived racism in social institutions	Black-White	Institutional racism subscale of the Index of Race-Related Stress-Brief Version (IRRS-B).[**]
Greer and Spalding, 2017	Perceived racism in socialinstitutions	Black-White	Institutional racism subscale of the Index of Race-Related Stress-Brief Version (IRRS-B).

Study	Domain	Comparison	Measure
Jacoby, et. al., 2017	Residential neighborhood/ housing	Black-White	2010 Census tract color category based on the 1937 Home Owner's Loan Corporation redlining map.
Krivo et al., 2009	Residential neighborhood/ housing	Black-White	Census tract socioeconomic disadvantage index and index of dissimilarity.
Lukachko et al., 2014	Political participation, socioeconomic status, criminal justice	Black-White	Relative proportions of Blacks to Whites in each state who were >age 18 and registered to vote, who actually voted, and who were elected to the state legislature; who were >age 16 and were employed, who were in executive or managerial positions, and who were in professional specialties; who were >25 and had attained a bachelor's level degree or higher; who were incarcerated (jails and prisons), felony disenfranchised, or serving a death sentence.
McCluney et al., 2017	Workplace environment	Black-White	Subjective (self-reported) and objective ratings of psychosocial workplace environment: opportunities for advancement, work recognized, autonomy, decision freedom, training support, supportive management.
Mendez et al., 2011	Residential neighborhood/ housing	Black-White	Redlining index (Black-White disparity in odds of mortgage loan denial by Census tract).
Mendez et al., 2014	Residential neighborhood/ housing	Black-White	Redlining index.

Table 2 (cont.)

Author(s)	Domain(s)	Racial ethnic comparisons	Measure(s) of structural racism[*]
Patler and Pirtle, 2017	Immigration and border enforcement	Latinx immigrant youth	Deferred Action for Childhood Arrivals (DACA) status.
Sabo et al., 2014	Immigration and border enforcement	US citizen and permanent residents of Mexican descent	Prevalence and type of perceived ethno racial profiling, frequency and location of sightings of immigration officials, and direct encounters with immigration officials, including immigration related detention.
Scott et al., 2014	Perceived racism in social institutions	Black–White	Adapted scale of Diaz et al., to assess men's experience of racism and homophobia in the past year.
Seaton, 2010	Perceived racism in social institutions	Black–White	Institutional racism subscale of the Index of Race-Related Stress (IRRS).
Vines and Baird, 2009	Perceived racism in social institutions	Black–White	Telephone-Administered Perceived Racism Scale (TPRS) items involving institutionalized forms of racism.[***]
Wallace et al., 2015	Socioeconomic status, criminal justice	Black–White	Relative proportions of Blacks to Whites in each state who were >age 16 and employed; who were >age 25 and had attained a bachelor's or higher degree; who were prison incarcerated.

Wallace et al., 2017	Socioeconomic status, criminal justice	Black-White	Relative proportions of Blacks to Whites in each state who were >age 16 and employed, employed in professional occupations; who were >age 25 and had attained a bachelor's or higher degree; Black to White ratios of median household income, prison incarceration and juvenile custody rates.

*   See Table 3 for methods used for quantifying measures of structural racism.

** The Index of Race-Related Stress is a 46-item instrument designed to measure race-related stress experienced by Black adults as a result of specific daily events of racism and discrimination. Race-related stress was defined as the occurrence and perceived magnitude of specific events of racism and discrimination that Blacks potentially experience in their daily lives (Lazarus, Richard S., and Susan Folkman. 1984. *Stress, Appraisal, and Coping*. New York: Springer Publishing).

*** The Perceived Racism Scale is a 20-item scale that measures how often people feel that others treat them badly or unfairly on the basis of race, ethnicity, gender, age, religion, physical appearance, sexual orientation, or other characteristics. The scale covers discrimination in different areas of life, including at school, at work, and in one's neighborhood. (Williams, D. R., Yu, Y., Jackson, J. S., and Anderson, N.B. 1997. Racial Differences in Physical and Mental Health: Socio-economic Status, Stress and Discrimination. *Journal of Health Psychology*, 2(3): 335–351).

Source: Adapted from Groos, Maya, Maeve Wallace, Rachel Hardeman and Katherine Theall. 2018. Measuring Inequity: A Systematic Review of Methods Used to Quantify Structural Racism. *Journal of Health Disparities Research and Practice*, 11(2): 190–206, at pp. 195–196.

indicators of structural racism, as compared with novel indicators, better explain racial disparities in birth outcomes. Chambers and colleagues point out that *racial segregation* is a key indicator of structural racism, and it is traditionally measured by spatial distributions between and among social groups across geographic regions using five indices:

(1) dissimilarity index (i.e., evenness of two social groups);
(2) isolation index (exposure/interaction between two social groups);
(3) concentration or delta index (concentration of one social group across a geographic region);
(4) centralization index (centralization of one social group to the center of a geographic region), and
(5) clustering index (the extent to which people from on social group reside in adjoining geographic regions; also see Massey and Denton, 1988).

Their study relies on three of these traditional indices: dissimilarity, isolation, and delta. Table 3 provides the measures and methods used to quantify structural racism for their study.

Chambers and colleagues also relied on two novel indicators of structural racism at the county level: Judicial treatment and political participation.[35] As seen in Table 4, judicial treatment refers to the ratio of Blacks and Whites incarcerated for a federal felony, and political participation refers to the ratio of Blacks and Whites elected to a County Board of Supervisors. These indices tend to be more commonly used in social sciences, including public administration. And, in the social sciences they may be viewed more as traditional rather than novel. In any case, the novel indicators did little to predict disparities between Black and White women in birth outcomes, but the traditional indices did uncover evidence of structural racism. Moreover, their traditional measures comport with the underlying premises of CRT. As Chambers and colleagues (2018: 967) argue, racial or residential "segregation indices aim to capture the aftermaths of enslavement of Africans through the use of collective action racism (i.e., institutionalized laws and legislation to separate Blacks from Whites) and centralized racism (i.e., an operative process used to maintain separation between Blacks and whites) to geographically separate Blacks from Whites and allocate resources accordingly."[36]

---

[35] Lukachko and colleagues (2014) used novel state-level indicators of structural racism across four areas: political participation, judicial treatment, educational attainment, and employment and job status.

[36] For additional quantitative studies that can help guide research in public administration via a CRT framework, see, e.g., Hicken, Kravitz-Wirtz, Durkee and Jackson (2018); Ford and Airhihenbuwa (2010).

Table 3 Methods used for quantifying structural racism

Structural racism measure	Data source(s)	Methodology in estimation
Historical Redline Color Category	1937 Home Owner's Loan Corporation, 2010 Census block shapefile	Imported the historical map image as a raster layer into ArcMap v.10.3, then aligned this layer with Census 2010 blocks. Blocks were assigned to one of five categories (green, blue, yellow, red, or not zoned) in which their center point (internal centroid) was located.
Redlining Indices	Home Mortgage Disclosure Act (HMDA) data available through the Federal Financial Institutions Examination Council's HMDA Loan Application Register	Mendez et al.(Mendez et al., 2011; Mendez et al., 2013, 2014): Multilevel logistic model to account for clustering of individual loans within census tracts, fit with a random intercept and random slope for race to estimate Black–White difference in log odds of loan denial controlling for loan amount, income, and gender of the applicant.
		Gee, 2008: Estimated an odds ratio for each tract including applicant's race and the ratio of load request to applicant income. Redlined areas operationalized as tracts where Asian home mortgage loan applications were disfavored by 40 percent in comparison to White applicants (OR>1.4).

Table 3 (cont.)

Structural racism measure	Data source(s)	Methodology in estimation
		Zhou et al., 2017: Integration of logistic regression models with the adaptive spatial filtering (ASF) approach.
Index of Dissimilarity	U.S. Census Bureau	$D = 0.5 * \sum_{i=1}^{n} |x_i/X - yi/Y|$ where x_i is the proportion of area i (census tract) that is Black, X is the proportion of the larger geographic unit (county) that is Black, y_i is the proportion of tract i that is White, Y is the proportion of the county that is White. D is the proportion of Blacks that would have to change their place of residence to achieve an even distribution of Whites and Blacks in the region (Chambers et al., 2017).
Isolation Index	American Community Survey, U.S. Census Bureau	$xPx* = \sum_{i=1}^{n} [(x_i/X)(x_i/t_i)]$ where x_i is the total Blacks in a census tract, t_i is the total population (Blacks + Whites) in a census tract, X is total Blacks in a county. xPx* represents the probability

		that Blacks will reside in the same subarea within a county as other Blacks. Scores range from 0 (complete integration) to 1 (complete segregation). (Chambers et al., 2017).
Delta Index	American Community Survey, U.S. Census Bureau	$$Del = \frac{1}{2}\sum_{i=1}^{n}\left[(x_i/X)(a_i/A)\right]$$ where x_i is the total Blacks in a census tract, X is the total Blacks in a county, a_i is the total land area in a census tract and A is the total land area in a county. Del represents the proportion of Blacks that would have to change their place of residence to achieve uniform density across a county. Scores range from 0 (complete integration) to 1 (complete segregation). (Chambers et al., 2017).
Neighborhood Deprivation Index	U.S. Census Bureau	Average z-scores of the extent of joblessness, professional or managerial occupations (reverse coded), high school graduates (reverse coded), female-headed families, secondary sector workers (those in the six occupations with the lowest average incomes), and poverty.
Relative Proportions of Blacks to Whites	U.S. Census Bureau, U.S. Department of Labor and Statistics, U.S. Department of Justice, Bureau of Justice Statistics	Ratio of Black to White population values for each indicator. Ratio values less than 1 indicate Blacks underrepresented; values greater than 1 indicate Blacks overrepresented.

Table 3 (cont.)

Structural racism measure	Data source(s)	Methodology in estimation
Psychosocial Workplace Environment	Department of Labor Occupational Information Network (O*NET), Health and Retirement Study (HRS)	Six measures of workplace environment scored between 1 and 5 summed and normalized to take values between 0 and 1, estimated separately among white and Black workers.

Sources: Adapted from Chambers, et. al. 2018. Testing the Association Between Traditional and Novel Indicators of County-Level Structural Racism and Birth Outcomes among Black and White Women. *Journal Racial and Ethnic Health Disparities*, 5(1): 966–977, and Groos, et. al. 2018. Measuring Inequity: A Systematic Review of Methods Used to Quantify Measuring Inequity: A Systematic Review of Methods Used to Quantify Structural Racism. *Journal of Health Disparities Research and Practice*, 11(2): 190–206.

Table 4 Description of measurement of novel indicators of structural racism items

Novel indicators of structural racism	Measure	Description	Data sources
Judicial treatment	Felony incarcerations	Ratio of Blacks/Whites at the county-level who are incarcerated for a felony	Center on Juvenile and Criminal Justice (2012)
Political participation: elected office	Racial composition of County Board of Supervisors	Ratio of Blacks/Whites who were elected to County Board of Supervisors	County Board of Supervisors websites (2016)

Source: Chambers, Brittany D., Jennifer Toller Erausquin, Amanda E. Tanner, Tracy R. Nichols and Shelly Brown-Jeffy. 2018. Testing the Association Between Traditional and Novel Indicators of County-Level Structural Racism and Birth Outcomes among Black and White Women. *Journal Racial and Ethnic Health Disparities*, 5(1): 966–977.

Another area to study CRT with quantitative methods is zoning policies, which falls in the domain of local government. As noted earlier, segregation by race in the United States is a primary source of structural and institutional racism. Discriminatory zoning policies adversely affect Black and Latinx families, sending them the message that unless they could afford a single-family home, they are not welcome in certain, primarily White communities. Racial zoning was struck down by the U.S. Supreme Court's 1917 *Buchanan* v. *Warley* decision, where Louisville, Kentucky's zoning policies explicitly prohibited Black people from living in White communities. Soon after, cities began implementing economic zoning policies that had the same effect (Kahlenberg, 2021). Most cities in the United States today have zoning laws that prohibit the construction of large multifamily units (e.g., duplexes, triplexes, and quads) on large swaths of available city property, which continues to discriminate against families of color (see Baca, McAnaney and Schuetz, 2019).

Research by Rothwell and Massey (2009: 780) questions the effects of zoning policies on segregation patterns. They begin by pointing out that "[t]hroughout the twentieth century, affluent Whites have taken political actions to separate themselves spatially from perceived out-groups – first Southern and Eastern European immigrants, then African-Americans, and most recently Hispanics, but always the lower classes." They argue that segregation patterns continue today because jurisdictions with low-density zoning are less likely to have Black residents than those without such regulations (also see Pendall, 2000). Low-density residential zoning creates and sustains neighborhoods with larger lot sizes, which allows primarily for single-family dwellings. As noted, these policies adversely affect families of color. Relying on census data and local regulatory indicators, Rothwell and Massey estimate a series of regression models to measure the effect of density zoning on Black segregation. They find that a strong, significant cross-sectional relationship between racial segregation and low-density zoning, even after controlling for such variables as other zoning policies and various city characteristics.

Certainly, there are a number of opportunities for applying quantitative methods via a CRT framework in public administration. Generating such research can help to promote our understanding of structural and institutional racism and its effects on creating inequalities in the areas of health, employment, criminal justice (especially policing), education, environmental justice, and other areas that intersect with public administration and policy.

CRT and Public Administration: Bridging Theory with Practice

Public administration is an applied field, where there is an expectation that theory will be translated into practice, which in turn will help to inform theory, and so on and so forth. CRT helps to keep the focus on equity while carrying out not only research but practice as well. As Ford and Airhihenbuwa (2010: S32)[37] point out, "Community engagement and critical self-reflection enrich research processes, while research based on the lived experiences of marginalized communities provides the communities with more meaningful data for their ongoing efforts toward collective self-improvement." They go on to say that addressing the policy and practice implications in the published research, and then disseminating the findings to relevant practitioner audiences is vital. Certainly, the works of Alexander and Stivers (2020) and Witt (2006) discussed earlier, point to the importance of doing so in the context of administrative practice.

In this vein, one useful theory here that emanates from CRT and is gaining popularity in public administration is Victor Ray's (2019a) "theory of racialized organizations." Ray draws heavily on CRT, as he seeks to bridge the subfields of race and organizational theory; that is, he theorizes organizations and racial progress through the lens of CRT. Because his focus is on meso-level organization, he asks what organizations can do to address racism. More specifically, especially in relation to public administration, Ray's focus is on how organizations, at the meso-level, are affected by macro-level policies and politics (e.g., from government) and micro-level behaviors of individuals (e.g., workers).[38] He contends that the racist systems and structures created by government and individual prejudice are filtered through organizations and suggests that organizations can moderate or change those racist structures and behaviors through their practices and policies.[39] Ray (2019b: online) recognizes that organizations themselves are the purveyors of racism, and are "central to the reproduction of the racial order as a whole." He states that "[o]rganizations distribute healthcare and education, and they organize policing and public safety." But he also argues that organizations will respond to "pressures from activists or markets" and are thereby "central to the changes in the racial order." In this sense, his work points

---

[37] Ford and Airhihenbuwa (2010) advanced the Public Health Critical Race Praxis (PHCRP) to support the application of CRT to public health research.

[38] Some use the term "macro-level" to explicitly refer to the broader issue of institutional and structural racism.

[39] History and experience tell us that organizations have done little if anything to change or moderate microlevel or institutional racism. For example, meso- and macro-level policies such as the use of merit continue to be relied upon by governments at every level. Merit suggests neutrality and equal playing fields, which are bureaucratic myths (see Portillo, Bearfield and Humphrey, 2020).

to the importance of how research can help to guide organizations in eradicating discrimination and racial animus.[40]

Earlier work by Ray and colleagues addressed the under-theorization of racial progress in our society (see, e.g.,Christian, Seamster, and Ray, 2019a; 2019b; Ray and Seamster, 2016). They draw on CRT and Afro-Pessimism[41] to argue that racism is the fundamental cause of social inequality. From this perspective, Ray and colleagues have worked to advance a theory to help explain continuity as well as change in racial inequality. Ray, Randolph, Underhill and Luke (2017), for example, suggest that CRT and Afro-Pessimism could be applied to diversity and labor market research. As they point out, diversity, as an individual value, has been framed from a White, middle-class perspective, which positions this group as a "different kind of white," one who is progressive and tolerant (p 152). Ray and colleagues suggest that a more accurate conception of diversity should rely on the perceptions of working- and lower-class Whites, despite the fact the media tends to portray this socioeconomic group as uniformly racist (some would contest the continued focus on Whites[42]). They suggest that research on working- and lower-class Whites might show that White women may be more tolerant of diversity compared to men who are middle class and White (see Bonilla-Silva, 2014).

Ray and colleagues go on to extol the significance of diversity from an organizational standpoint: "Diversity also improves business outcomes; employees of color help businesses expand into emerging markets via the identification, design, and marketing of products that appeal to a broader demographic of consumers ... In universities, diversity is thought to enrich student learning, particularly for whites, by adding color and complexity to their academic experience" (Ray, et. al., 2017: 152).[43] They suggest that to better

---

[40] Although Ray does not offer qualitative or quantitative methodological suggestions here, his work suggests that both qualitative and quantitative CRMs can be applied to classic sociological questions, which can provide insights for public administration research as well.

[41] Afro-pessimism posits that the State construes Blacks as internal enemies of civil society, thus justifying society's dependence on antiblack violence (see, for example, Douglass et.al., 2018).

[42] Some have questioned the "power" that determines or conceptualizes diversity, arguing that Whites should not take central stage. Diversity, notwithstanding class, cannot be exclusively about Whites, especially White men. To do so, reflects what Swan (2017, 547) refers to as "collective white ignorance." Also see Pullen, et. al. (2017), (2017) and Grimes (2002) who stresses the importance of "de-centering whiteness."

[43] Traditional critical race theorists might be skeptical of Ray's work in a vein similar to their critiques of affirmative action, as discussed earlier in the text. They may raise concerns with the slow pace and effectiveness of diversity programs in creating diversity and ultimately in creating change. See, for example, Hutchison (2008: 1097) who argues that this nation's history "with racist oppression and apartheid-like exclusion .... cannot be rescued by diversity rhetoric." Similarly, Iverson (2007: 586) finds in her study that diversity reinforces predominant images of people of color: "as outsiders, at-risk victims, commodities, and change agents. These discourses coalesce to produce realities that situate people of color as outsiders to the institution, at risk

understand diversity from an organizational perspective, perceptions of people of color are needed as well as further exploration of a White-centered organizational culture. They go on to say that the value of racial diversity should focus not on the value it adds to White individuals and organizations, but rather how it promotes a quality of life for people of color.

In terms of labor market research Ray and colleagues (2017: 153) argue that "CRT challenges the narrative of smooth economic mobility, and Afropessimism highlights the conditions that make black economic immobility distinct." They recommend the use of audit studies to address labor market inequality. Audit studies are a type of experimental method used to test for discriminatory behavior, where researchers can control for human capital and race, and thus examine more closely discrimination on the part of, for example, employers. Pager (2007) in her classic audit study relied on a field experiment where she matched up pairs of young Black and White men, randomly assigned them criminal records, then sent them on real job searches throughout the city of Milwaukee. All applicants had similar qualities, except for their criminal record. She found that young Black men without a criminal record were less likely to receive a callback as compared to White men just out of prison.

This type of audit study in public administration, however, conducted on government organizations, would face challenges in meeting a university's Institutional Review Board (IRB) regulations especially around ethical behavior. Thus, online experiments may be an option, providing they are theoretically based and cognizant of the institutional contexts of public administration (Bertelli and Riccucci, 2020). Certainly, CRT would fulfill this need.

In sum, Ray's "theory of racialized organizations" may inform public administration research as its focus on meso-level organization directs organizations to consider those policies and practices that will assist in jettisoning racism; as noted earlier, however, until government organizations abandon the use of merit practices and policies, this seems unlikely. In addition, addressing the policy and practice implications in CRT studies is important. Certainly, several journals in public administration help to bridge theory and practice (e.g., *Public Administration Review*, *Review of Public Personnel Administration*, *Public Budgeting & Finance*, *Public Integrity* and *Public Performance & Management Review*, to name a few). This could help identify the policy changes needed to remedy structural racism in organizations, and at least

---

before and during participation in education, and dependent on the university for success in higher education." She concludes that "well-intentioned attempts to create a more inclusive campus may unwittingly reinforce practices that support exclusion and inequity" (ibid). Also see Grimes (2002), who argues that focusing on Whiteness has led to only superficial organizational change and it vigorously upholds White privilege.

communicate to policymakers the importance of paying special attention to factors that work to improve conditions for specific racial and ethnic groups.

Conclusion

The voices of Blacks, Latinx, and other persons of color have been absent in the history of public administration. The field has not explored whether there were persons of color early on studying or practicing public administration, even in its initial or inchoate capacities (e.g., civic engineering and city planning).[44] The same can be said for political science; but, at least the first Black American to receive a PhD in political science was identified as Ralph Johnson Bunche in 1934, from Harvard University (Woodard and Preston, 1985).[45] Some political scientists, including McClain and colleagues (2016), for example, explored the reasons why it took so long for scholars of race, ethnicity, and politics to be recognized in the field and for the legitimacy of studying race and racial politics in political science. They state that the

> answer to this question, we believe, lies in the historical roots of the discipline ... [and] the complex relationship between racial ideologies and the development of the discipline of political science in the United States. Using a genealogical analysis, we analyze the racist origins of the discipline that arose from the work and attitudes of one of the founders of American political science, John W. Burgess. In an effort to legitimize political science as an empirical field rooted in the scientific method, Burgess and other prominent early political scientists turned to existing "scientific" notions of race. The racial ideologies that spurred the early development of political science continue to influence the ways in which issues of race and ethnicity are embraced and understood within the discipline today and contribute to its lack of diversity (McClain, et. al., 2016: 467; also see Rich, 2007; Smith, 2018).

Likewise, we may look to the racist legacy of one of the founders of public administration, Woodrow Wilson, as discussed earlier in the text, to discern the long gestation for the legitimacy of investigating race issues in public adminis-tration (also see Gooden, 2014; Lehr, 2015). Today, it is important to examine theories as well as practices that are significant to matters of race and ethnicity as well as to gender and gender identity. This requires public administration scholars to go beyond traditional topics and substantive areas to include others that are contemporary and relevant to the field. CRT is one example here. It is

---

[44] Indeed, we do not know the role that Black Americans were even allowed to play in general in our society. Some contributions have been documented, but have been virtually erased. One example can be seen in the persistent denial of the important role that Blacks played in building the Southern economic infrastructure.

[45] W. E. B. Du Bois was the first Black person to receive a Ph.D. from Harvard; in History in 1895.

particularly important when we consider the fact that the economic and class divide between Blacks and Whites has become exponentially greater since the early twentieth century, and has grown significantly since 2020. Racism at the individual level holds some explanatory power here, but the primary determinant of not only social, political, and economic inequality of Blacks but also of White supremacy is institutional and structural racism. Two common interests of CRT research is (1) an understanding how White supremacy, institutional racism, and the subordination of people of color have been created and maintained in America, and (2) working to ameliorate racism and change the bond that exists between law, public policy, racist practices, and racial power (Sung and Coleman, 2019).

Incorporating a CRT lens into public administration requires the field in part to return to its normative roots. The compassionate, humanistic (read "art") side of public administration asks us to question, for example, why does the abhorrent problem of police violence against Black and Brown persons continue in our society? What can practitioners of public administration (e.g., our MPA graduates) do to help diminish and end this problem? It is important for students of public administration to have frank discussions about why, in 2021, this perversity remains intractable and prevalent.

As addressed here, a CRT lens is pertinent for qualitative and quantitative studies, although qualitative research can provide a richer contextual framework for addressing structural and institutional racism in public administration. The elephant in the room here, of course, is the norms of academia for the social sciences, namely the need to publish copiously in order to be tenured. In short, there are enormous institutional norms and pressures to publish. Sound, robust qualitative research is much more time consuming than quantitative research. Thus, untenured scholars are motivated to focus their energies on quantitative research – it is expedient and goal-oriented. But if a high premium is placed on serious, consequential scholarship on institutional and structural racism in public administration, the norms of tenure in our field need to shift so that sound qualitative research is considered just as significant as quantitative research. This is a matter of reevaluating priorities in our field, one that for some time has placed a high value on social equity.

Appendix

Evaluating Quantitative Public Health Studies from a CRT Perspective

First Author, Study Year, HINTS Dataset[*]	Objective	Key Findings	CRT Considerations
(Agurs-Collins et al., 2015) HINTS 4, cycle 3 (2013)	To assess the prevalence of awareness of direct to consumer (DTC) genetic testing, identify sources of information regarding DTC genetic testing; and identify demographic, cognitive, and behavioral correlates of awareness of DTC genetic testing.	Income was the only demographic variable significantly associated with awareness of DTC genetic testing. Participants with annual incomes of $99,999 or less had lower odds of being aware of DTC genetic testing (ORs ranging from 0.46–0.61) than did those participants with an income of $100,000 or more. None of the predisposing factors defined by the framework (fatalism, worry, perceived risk, mortality salience and perceived ambiguity about cancer prevention) were found to be significantly associated with DTC testing awareness but awareness was positively	Race and ethnicity are described as distinct background factors in the adapted conceptual framework but no associations with DTC awareness were observed. Racial and ethnic income inequality represent a persistently entangled disparity.

(cont.)

First Author, Study Year, HINTS Dataset[*]	Objective	Key Findings	CRT Considerations
		associated with enabling factors like internet use and cancer information-seeking behaviors. A significant association between DTC awareness and a measure of objective numeracy was observed.	
(Arora et al., 2008) HINTS 4, cycle 1 (2011)	To evaluate "patient-centeredness" or how often (from the perspective of the patient) providers engaged patients in Patient Centered Care (PCC) by fostering healing relationships, exchanging information, facilitating decision-making, responding to emotions, enabling self-management, and managing uncertainty.	Although 45–61% of the population reported that they "always" received PCC, 25% reported they rarely received help dealing with uncertainty about their health care, 23% reported their providers never paid attention to their emotions, 18% were rarely involved in decision-making as much as they wanted, and 10% reported being unable to ask their health-related questions during medical visits; they leave the	Racial characteristics of the population reporting "low patient-centeredness" are not provided but may be important to employ the six-function framework of PCC in environments enabled by breast cancer genomic medicine.

office not understanding what they need to do to take care of their health care.		
(Krakow et al., 2017) HINTS 5, cycle 1 (2017)	To determine prevalence of genetic testing awareness and to assess uptake of genetic tests in the general population.	Black respondents (OR: 0.49, CI: .31, .78) were less likely be aware of genetic testing, compared to non-Hispanic White respondents. Individuals with household incomes over $75,000 were more likely to report awareness of genetic tests, compared to the lowest household income category (OR: 1.72, CI: 1.13, 2.60). The most commonly reported types of tests were ancestry tests (11.11%), paternity tests (8.97%), DNA fingerprinting (8.51%), and Cystic Fibrosis carrier tests (6.87%). Only 5.36% had undergone at least one	Genetic testing awareness was determined by a yes to the following question, "Doctors use DNA tests to analyze someone's DNA for health reasons. Have you heard or read about this type of genetic test?" The question injects a bias because many may be aware of ancestry and paternity tests but may not refer to them as genetic tests or they may not be aware that doctors use genetic tests for health reasons. Only those who answered "yes" to genetic testing awareness were also

(cont.)

First Author, Study Year, HINTS Dataset[*]	Objective	Key Findings	CRT Considerations
		cancer-related test: 4.88% reported BRCA testing, and even fewer (2.52%) had undergone testing for Lynch Syndrome.	asked about the types of genetic tests they had ever received.
Kushalnagar et al., 2019) HINTS- ASL HINTS 5, cycle 1 (2017)	To comparatively investigate genetic testing awareness among Deaf and the Hearing women and their use of eHealth platforms.	Deaf women who had not heard of genetic testing were more likely to self-identify as Black. The racial disparity for awareness of genetic testing was significantly higher among Deaf women compared to their hearing peers ($\chi^2 = 20.90$, p < 0.001).	Racial disparities may be more challenging when individuals represent multiple (or intersectional) disparity populations. This study showed an association between educational attainment and genetic testing awareness, which may indicate a need for ASL health education materials that are understood at a sixth grade level.

| (Quillin, 2016) HINTS 4, cycle 3 (2013) | To explore lifestyle risk factors and uptake of genetic testing for BRCA or Lynch Syndrome. | About 80% of respondents reported White race. Most (about 65%) had at least some college education. There were no differences in race or education according to genetic testing status. Two leading lifestyle risk factors for cancer are obesity and smoking. Over half of the respondents reported having a BMI of equal to or greater than 25 kg/m^2 (58%), which indicates being overweight or obese, and 24% identified themselves as current smokers. "Seeking genetic testing for cancer risk does not necessarily mean that the patient has also made lifestyle changes to address her or his cancer risk." | The analysis was stratified as White or non-White. There is no discussion of disparities specific to Black populations. Also, the study demystifies the notion that genetic testing awareness equates with health behaviors and cancer risk-reducing lifestyle factors. |

First Author, Study Year, HINTS Dataset*	Objective	Key Findings	CRT Considerations
(Roberts et al., 2018) HINTS 4, cycle 3 (2013)	To examine the association between receiving genetic information from trusted sources and genetic test uptake within a sample of US adults to determine if people trust their genetic testing information sources, and if trust is associated with uptake.	Overall, individuals with missing data for the dependent variable and primary independent variables had lower education and income and were Black, Hispanic, or female (data not shown). However, those receiving cancer-related genetic testing tended to be female and were more likely to have a personal history of cancer compared to those who did not receive testing. Respondents reported that they trusted information from health professionals the most but were less likely to hear about genetic testing from them. More often	When data is missing, Black women may not be adequately represented in the study population and results are conveyed without distinguishers for race and ethnicity. Backward elimination was used and only independent variables that were significant were used in the final regression model.

Study	Aim	Results	
		respondents heard about genetic testing from the television, which happened to be a less trusted source.	The results underscore the relationships between race, education, income, and perceived numeracy.
		Increased levels of trust for genetic information sources were associated with increased predicted probability of uptake, only if the respondent had a personal history of cancer.	Although many Americans (30%) score below the lowest numeracy proficiency level 1, numeracy among racial and ethnic minority and low-income populations show an even greater disparity. Also,
(Ross et al., 2018) HINTS 2007	To evaluate the relationships between three self-reported, perceived low numeracy items and cancer-related knowledge, beliefs, and affect.	The three perceived numeracy measures were associated with many of the demographic characteristics.	
		Respondents with low numeracy understanding were more likely to be of ethnic/racial minority status ($X^2 = 18.3$, $P < 0.001$), report lower household income ($X^2 = 18.3$, $P < 0.001$), have lower educational attainment (X^2	

First Author, Study Year, HINTS Dataset[*]	Objective	Key Findings	CRT Considerations
		= 58.3, $P < 0.001$), and be more likely to prefer Spanish ($X^2 = 9.9$, $P = 0.002$).

Respondents with low numeracy comfort were more likely to be female ($X^2 = 10.0$, $P = 0.002$), be of ethnic/racial minority status ($X^2 = 11.1$, $P = 0.010$), report lower household income ($X^2 = 49.4$, $P < 0.001$), have lower educational attainment ($X^2 = 49.4$, $P < 0.001$), and be more likely to prefer Spanish ($X^2 = 9.3$, $P = 0.002$).

After controlling for most demographics, low numeracy comfort remained significantly associated with fatalism (OR | the discomfort with numeracy is aligned with increased fatalism, overload and worry. To fully understand the essence of attitudinal factors, one must view them within the broadest historical and sociocultural context to accurately measure impact. |

1.63, 95% CI 1.23±2.14, $P < 0.001$), information overload (OR 2.37, 95% CI 1.79±3.13, $P < 0.001$), low prevention knowledge (OR 1.79, 95% CI 1.32±2.42, $P < 0.001$), and high frequency of worry (OR 1.68, 95% CI 1.14±2.49, $P = 0.01$). Respondents with low numeracy use were more likely to report lower household income ($X^2 = 10.4$, $P = 0.030$), and have lower educational attainment ($X^2 = 10.2$, $P = 0.020$).

---

* Refers to Health Information National Trends Survey (HINTS), the biennial, cross-sectional survey of a nationally-representative sample of American adults collected by the National Cancer Institute.

Source: Gerido, Lynette Hammond. 2020. Racial Disparities in Breast Cancer and Genomic Uncertainty: A QuantCrit Mini-Review. *Open Information Science*, 4(1): 39–57.

References

Adams, Char. 2021. How Trump Ignited the Fight Over Critical Race Theory in Schools. May 10. www.nbcnews.com/news/nbcblk/how-trump-ignited-fight-over-critical-race-theory-schools-n1266701, accessed June 15, 2021.

Alexander, Jennifer. 1997. Avoiding the Issue: Racism and Administrative Responsibility in Public Administration. *American Review of Public Administration*, 27(4): 343–361.

Alexander, Jennifer and Camilla Stivers. 2020. Racial Bias: A Buried Cornerstone of the Administrative State. *Administration & Society*, 52(10): 1470–1490.

Alexander, Jennifer and Camilla Stivers. 2010. An Ethic of Race for Public Administration. *Administrative Theory & Praxis*, 32(4): 578–597.

Baca, Alex, Patrick McAnaney and Jenny Schuetz. 2019. "Gentle" Density Can Save Our Neighborhoods. December 4. www.brookings.edu/research/gentle-density-can-save-our-neighborhoods/, accessed June 21, 2021.

Baldwin, James. 1961. *Nobody Knows My Name: More Notes of a Native Son*. New York: Dial Press.

Banks, James A. 1995. The Historical Reconstruction of Knowledge about Race: Implications for Transformative Teaching. *Educational Researcher*, 24(2): 15–25.

Barden, Jamie, William W. Maddux, Richard E. Petty and Marilynn B. Brewer. 2004. Contextual Moderation of Racial Bias: The Impact of Social Roles on Controlled and Automatically Activated Attitudes. *Journal of Personality and Social Psychology*, 87(1): 5–22.

Basford, Tessa E., Lynn R. Offermann and Tara S. Behrend. 2014. Do You See What I See? Perceptions of Gender Microaggressions in the Workplace. *Psychology of Women Quarterly*, 38(3): 340–349.

Bearfield, Domonic A. 2020. Invited Essay. *Management Matters*, 18(2): 3. The Public Management Research Association Newsletter, http://pmranet.org/wp-content/uploads/Management-Matters-V-18-2.pdf, accessed January 18, 2021.

Bearfield, Domonic A. 2009. Equity at the Intersection: Public Administration and the Study of Gender. *Public Administration Review*, 69(3): 383–386.

Bearfield, Domonic A., Nicole Humphrey and Shannon Portillo. 2021. The Myth of Representation: Identity and Workplace Expectations in Public Administration. In, Bearfield, Domonic A., Nicole Humphrey & Shannon Portillo (eds.), *The Myth of Bureaucratic Neutrality: An Examination of Merit and Representation* (New York: Routledge), forthcoming.

Bell, Derrick. 2000. Affirmative Action: Another Instance of Racial Workings in the United States. *The Journal of Negro Education*, 69(1/2): 145–149.

Bell, Derrick A. Jr. 1995. Who's Afraid of Critical Race Theory? *University of Illinois Law Review*, 4: 893–910.

Bell, Derrick A. Jr. 1992. *Faces at the Bottom of the Well: The Permanence of Racism*. New York: Basic Books.

Bell, Derrick. 1989. Xerces and the Affirmative Action Mystique. *George Washington Law Review*, 57: 1595–1613.

Bell, Derrick. 1987. *And We Are Not Saved: The Elusive Quest for Racial Justice*. New York: Basic Books.

Benz, Terressa A. 2019. Toxic Cities: Neoliberalism and Environmental Racism in Flint and Detroit Michigan. *Critical Sociology*, 45(1): 49–62.

Bertelli, Anthony M. and Norma M. Riccucci. 2020. What Is Behavioral Public Administration Good for? *Public Administration Review*, early view, http://doi.org/10.1111/puar.13283.

Blessett, Brandi. 2020. Urban Renewal and "Ghetto" Development in Baltimore: Two Sides of the Same Coin. *American Review of Public Administration*, 50(8): 838–850.

Bliss, Catherine. 2012. *Race Decoded: The Genomic Fight for Social Justice*. Palo Alto, CA: Stanford University Press.

Bonilla-Silva, Eduardo. 2015. More than Prejudice: Restatement, Reflections, and New Directions in Critical Race Theory. *Sociology of Race and Ethnicity*, 1(1): 73–87.

Bonilla-Silva, Eduardo. 2014. *Racism without Racists: Colorblind Racism and the Persistence of Racial Inequality in America*, 4th ed. Lanham, MD: Rowman & Littlefield.

Brown v. *Board of Education*, 347 U.S. 483 (1954).

Brown, Dorothy A. 2003. *Critical Race Theory: Cases, Materials, and Problems*. Berkeley, CA: West Academic.

Brunson, Rod K. 2007. "Police Don't Like Black People:" African-American Young Men's Accumulated Police Experiences. *Criminology & Public Policy*, 6(1): 71–101.

Buchanan v. *Warley*, 245 U.S. 60 (1917).

Campbell, Jacquelyn. C. and Sheila Bunting. 1991. Voices and Paradigms: Perspectives on Critical and Feminist Theory in Nursing. *Advances in Nursing Science*, 13(3): 1–15.

Carbado, Devon W. and Daria Roithmayr. 2014. Critical Race Theory Meets Social Science. *Annual Review of Law and Social Science*, 10: 149–167.

Chambers, Brittany D., Jennifer Toller Erausquin, Amanda E. Tanner, Tracy R. Nichols and Shelly Brown-Jeffy. 2018. Testing the Association between

Traditional and Novel Indicators of County Level Structural Racism and Birth Outcomes among Black and White Women. *Journal Racial and Ethnic Health Disparities*, 5(1): 966–977.

Chapman, Rachel R. and Jean R. Berggren. 2005. Radical Contextualization: Contributions to an Anthropology of Racial/Ethnic Health Disparities. *Health*, 9(2): 145–167.

Chow, Denise. 2020. Why "I Can't Breathe" is Resonating with Environmental Activists. June 10. www.nbcnews.com/science/environment/why-i-can-t-breathe-resonating-environmental-justice-activists-n1228561, accessed January 21, 2021.

Christian, Michelle, Louise Seamster and Victor Ray. 2019a. New Directions in Critical Race Theory and Sociology: Racism, White Supremacy, and Resistance. *American Behavioral Scientist*, 63(13): 1731–1740.

Christian, Michelle, Louise Seamster and Victor Ray. 2019b. Critical Race Theory and Empirical Sociology. *American Behavioral Scientist*: 1–8.

Correll, Joshua, Bernadette Park, Charles M. Judd, Bernd Wittenbrink, Melody S. Sadler and Tracie Keesee. 2007. Across the Thin Blue Line: Police Officers and Racial Bias in the Decision to Shoot. *Journal of Personality and Social Psychology*, 92(6): 1006–1023.

Covarrubias, Alejandro, Pedro E. Nava, Argelia Lara, Rebeca Burciaga, Verónica N. Vélez and Daniel G. Solórzano. 2018. Critical Race Quantitative Intersections: A Testimonio Analysis. *Race Ethnicity and Education*, 21(2): 253–273.

Covarrubias, Alejandro and Verónica Vélez. 2013. Critical Race Quantitative Intersectionality. In Marvin Lynn and Adrienne D. Dixson (eds.), *Handbook of Critical Race Theory in Education*. New York: Routledge, pp. 270–285.

Coyle, Michael. 2010. Notes on the Study of Language: Towards Critical Race Criminology. *Western Criminology Review*, 11(1): 11–19.

Crenshaw, Kimberlé. 1996. *Critical Race Theory: The Key Writings that Formed the Movement*. New York: New Press.

Crenshaw, Kimberlé W. 1988. Race, Reform, and Retrenchment: Transformation and Legitimation in Anti-discrimination Law. *Harvard Law Review*, 101: 1331–1387.

Crenshaw, Kimberlé, Neil Gotanda, Garry Peller and Kendall Thomas (eds.). 1995. *Critical Race Theory: The Key Writings that Formed the Movement*. New York: New Press.

Cross, Rebekah Israel. 2018. Can Critical Race Theory Enhance the Field of Public Health? A Student's Perspective. *Ethnicity and Disease*, 28

(Suppl1): 267–270. www.ncbi.nlm.nih.gov/pmc/articles/PMC6092171/, accessed December 18, 2020.

Cunneen, Chris and Juan Marcellus Tauri. 2019. Indigenous Peoples, Criminology, and Criminal Justice. *Annual Review of Criminology*, 2(1): 359–381.

D'Agostino, Maria J. and Helisse Levine (eds.). 2011. *Women in Public Administration: Theory and Practice*. Sudbury, MA: Jones & Bartlett Learning.

Darling-Hammond, Linda. 2007. Race, Inequality and Educational Accountability: The Irony of No Child Left Behind. *Race Ethnicity and Education*, 10(3): 245–260.

Dasgupta, Nilanjana and Anthony G. Greenwald. 2001. On the Malleability of Automatic Attitudes: Combating Automatic Prejudice with Images of Admired and Disliked Individuals. *Journal of Personality and Social Psychology*, 81(5): 800–814.

Delgado, Richard. 1995. *Rodrigo Chronicles: Conversations about Race in America*. New York: New York University Press.

Delgado, Richard and Jean Stefancic. 2017. *Critical Race Theory: An Introduction*, 3rd ed. New York: New York University Press.

Delgado, Richard and Jean Stefancic. 2000. *Critical Race Theory: The Cutting Edge*. Philadelphia: Temple University Press.

Delgado, Richard and Jean Stefancic. 1993. Critical Race Theory: A Bibliography. *Virginia Law Review*, 79(2): 461–516.

Dickinson, Elizabeth. 2012. Addressing Environmental Racism through Storytelling: Toward an Environmental Justice Narrative Framework. *Communication, Culture and Critique*, 5(1): 57–74.

Douglass, Patrice, Selamawit D. Terrefe and Frank B. Wilderson. 2018. Afro-Pessimism. *Oxford Bibliographies*, August 28. www.oxfordbibliogra phies.com/view/document/obo-9780190280024/obo-9780190280024-0056.xml, accessed January 27, 2021.

Du Bois, W. E. B. (2007). *The Philadelphia Negro: A Social Study*. New York : Oxford University Press. (Originally published by the University of Pennsylvania Press in 1899).

Ferber, Abby. 2007. The Construction of Black Masculinity: White Supremacy Now and Then. *Journal of Sport & Social Issues*, 31(1):11–24.

Ford, Chandra L. and Collins O. Airhihenbuwa. 2010. The Public Health Critical Race Methodology: Praxis for Antiracism Research. *Social Science & Medicine*, 71(8): 1390–1398.

Frederickson, H. George. 1971. Toward a New Public Administration. In Frank Marini (ed.), *Toward a New Public Administration: The Minnowbrook Perspective*. Scranton, PA: Chandler, pp. 309–331.

1974. Social Equity and Public Administration, *Public Administration Review*, 34(1): 1–2.

1980. *New Public Administration*. Tuscaloosa: University of Alabama Press.

1990. Public administration and Social Equity. *Public Administration Review*, 50(2): 228–237.

Garcia, Nichole M., Nancy López and Verónica N. Vélez. 2017. QuantCrit: Rectifying Quantitative Methods Through Critical Race Theory. *Race Ethnicity and Education*, 21(2): 149–157.

García, Jennifer Jee-Lyn and Mienah Zulfacar Sharif. 2015. Black Lives Matter: A Commentary on Racism and Public Health. *American Journal of Public Health*, 105(8): e27–e30.

Gerido, Lynette Hammond. 2020. Racial Disparities in Breast Cancer and Genomic Uncertainty: A QuantCrit Mini-Review. *Open Information Science*, 4(1): 39–57.

Gilbert, K. L., and Ray, R. 2016. Why Police Kill Black Males with Impunity. *Journal of Urban Health*, 93(S1): 122–140.

Gillborn, David, Paul Warmington and Sean Demack. 2018. QuantCrit: Education, Policy, 'Big Data' and Principles for a Critical Race Theory of Statistics. *Race Ethnicity and Education*, 21(2): 158–179.

Gooden, Susan T. *Race and Social Equity: A Nervous Area of Government*. NY: Routledge, 2014.

Greenberg, David F. 2014. Studying New York City's Crime Decline: Methodological Issues. *Justice Quarterly* 31(1): 154–188.

Groos, Maya, Maeve Wallace, Rachel Hardeman and Katherine Theall. 2018. Measuring Inequity: A Systematic Review of Methods Used to Quantify Structural Racism. *Journal of Health Disparities Research and Practice*, 11(2): 190–206.

Hamilton, Charles. 1973. Full Employment as a Viable Issue. In, Andrew F. Brimmer (ed.), *When the Marching Stopped: An Analysis of Black Issues in the 70s*. New York: The National Urban League, 87–91.

Hamilton, James T. 1995. Testing for Environmental Racism: Prejudice, Profits, Political Power? *Journal of Policy Analysis and Management*, 14(1): 107–132.

Hanna, Alex, Emily Denton, Andrew Smart and Jamila Smith-Loud. 2020. Towards a Critical Race Methodology in Algorithmic Fairness. *Proceedings of the 2020 Conference on Fairness, Accountability, and Transparency*. January 2020: 501–512.

Harris, David A. 2002. *Profiles in Injustice: Why Racial Profiling Cannot Work*. New York : New Press.

Headley, Andrea M. and James E. Wright II. 2020. Is Representation Enough? Racial Disparities in Levels of Force and Arrests by Police. *Public Administration Review*, 80(6): 1051–1062.

Hesse-Biber, Sharlene Nagy (ed). 2014. *Feminist Research Practice: A Primer.* 2nd ed. Thousand Oaks: Sage, .

Heynen Nikolas C. 2003. The Scalar Production of Injustice Within the Urban Forest. *Antipode*, 35(5): 980–998.

Heynen, Nikolas C., Harold A. Perkins and Parama Roy. 2006. The Political Ecology of Uneven Urban Green Space: The Impact of Political Economy on Race and Ethnicity in Producing Environmental Inequality in Milwaukee. *Urban Affairs Review*, 42(1): 3–25.

Hicken, Margaret T., Nicole Kravitz-Wirtz, Myles Durkee, and James S. Jackson. 2018. Racial inequalities in health: Framing future research. *Social Science & Medicine*, 199: 11–18.

Hochschild, Jennifer L. 2005. Race and Class in Political Science. *Michigan Journal of Race and Law*, 11(1) : 99–114.

Hogarth, R. A. 2017. *Medicalizing Blackness: Making Racial Difference in the Atlantic World, 1780-1840.* Chapel Hill, NC: University of North Carolina Press.

Holifield, Ryan. 2009. Actor-Network Theory as a Critical Approach to Environmental Justice: A Case against Synthesis with Urban Political Ecology. *Antipode*, 41(4): 637–658.

Holland, Paul W. 1986. Statistics and Causal Inference. *Journal of the American Statistical Association*, 81(396): 945–970.

hooks, bell. 2000. *Feminist Theory: From Margin to Center.* Cambridge, MA: South End Press.

hooks, bell. 1995. *Killing Rage: Ending Racism.* New York: Henry Holt and Company.

hooks, bell. 1981. *Ain't I a Woman: Black Women and Feminism.* Cambridge, MA: South End Press.

Huang, Hong, Bénédicte Apouey and James E. Andrews. 2014. Racial and Ethnic Disparities in Awareness of Cancer Genetic Testing Among Online Users: Internet Use, Health Knowledge, and Socio-Demographic Correlates. *Journal of Consumer Health on the Internet*, 18(1),15–30.

Hutchinson, Janet R. 2002. En-Gendering Democracy. *Administrative Theory & Praxis*, 24(4): 721–738.

Hutchinson, Janet. 2001. Multigendering PA: Anti-administration, Anti-blues. *Administrative Theory & Praxis*, 23(4): 589–604.

Hutchinson, Janet R. and Mann, Hollie S. 2004. Feminist Praxis: Administering for a Multicultural, Multigendered. *Administrative Theory & Praxis*, 26 (1): 79–95.

Hutchinson, Janet R. and Mann, Hollie S. 2006. Gender Anarchy and the Future of Feminism in Public Administration. *Administrative Theory & Praxis*, 28(3): 399–417.

Hutchison, Harry G. 2008. Moving Forward? Diversity as a Paradox? A Critical Race View. *Catholic University Law Review*, 57(4): 1059–1098.

Iverson, Susan VanDeventer. 2007. Camouflaging Power and Privilege: A Critical Race Analysis of University Diversity Policies. *Educational Administration Quarterly*, 43(5): 586–611.

Johnson, Richard. 2017. Hamilton's Deracialization: Barack Obama's Racial Politics in Context. *Du Bois Review*, 14(2): 621–638.

Jones, Camara Phyllis. 2002. Confronting Institutionalized Racism. *Phylon*, 50 (1/2): 7–22.

Jones, D. Marvin. 1998. 'We're All Stuck Here for a While:' Law and the Social Construction of the Black Male, 24 *Journal of Contemporary Law* 35. https://repository.law.miami.edu/cgi/viewcontent.cgi?article=1362&context=fac_articles, accessed January 19, 2021.

Jones, T., McCarthy, A. M., Kim, Y., and Armstrong, K. 2017. Predictors of BRCA1/2 Genetic Testing among Black Women with Breast Cancer: A Population-Based Study. *Cancer Medicine*, 6(7): 1787–1798.

Kahlenberg, Richard D. 2021. Tearing Down the Walls: How the Biden Administration and Congress Can Reduce Exclusionary Zoning. April 18. https://production-tcf.imgix.net/app/uploads/2021/04/20160945/Tearing-Down-the-Walls_-How-the-Biden-Administration-and-Congress-Can-Reduce-Exclusionary-Zoning_.pdf, accessed June 21, 2021.

Kang, Jerry, et.al. 2012. Implicit Bias in the Courtroom. *UCLA Law Review*. 59 (5): 1124–86.

Krakow, M., Ratcliff, C. L., Hesse, B. W., and Greenberg-Worisek, A. J. 2017. Assessing Genetic Literacy Awareness and Knowledge Gaps in the US population: Results from the Health Information National Trends Survey. *Public Health Genomics*, 20(6): 343–348.

Krieger, Nancy. 2012. Methods for the Scientific Study of Discrimination and Health: An Ecosocial Approach. *American Journal Public Health*, 102(5): 936–944.

Krieger, Nancy. 1999. Embodying Inequality: A Review of Concepts, Measures, and Methods for Studying Health Consequences of Discrimination. *International Journal of Health Services*, 29(2): 295–352.

Kurtz, Hilda E. 2009. Acknowledging the Racial State: An Agenda for Environmental Justice Research. *Antipode*, 41(4): 684–704.

Kushalnagar, P., Holcomb, J., and Sadler, G. R. (2019). Genetic Testing and eHealth Usage Among Deaf Women. *Journal of Genetic Counseling*, 28 (5): 933–939.

Ladson-Billings, Gloria J. 1999. Preparing Teachers for Diverse Student Populations: A Critical Race Theory Perspective. *Review of Research in Education*, 24(1999): 211–247.

Leahy, Ian and Yaryna Serkez. 2021. Since When Have Trees Existed Only for Rich Americans? *New York Times*, June 30. www.nytimes.com/inter active/2021/06/30/opinion/environmental-inequity-trees-critical-infra structure.html, accessed July 1, 2021.

Lee, Hugh, Mark Learmonth and Nancy Harding. 2008. Queer(Y)Ing Public Administration. *Public Administration*, 86(1): 149–167.

Lehr, Dick. 2015. The Racist Legacy of Woodrow Wilson. *The Atlantic*, November 27. www.theatlantic.com/politics/archive/2015/11/wilson-leg acy-racism/417549/, accessed February 8, 2021.

Liu, Helena. 2017. Undoing Whiteness: The Dao of Anti-racist Diversity Practice. *Gender, Work and Organization*, 24(5): 457–471.

López, Gerardo R. 2001. Re-Visiting White Racism in Educational Research: Critical Race Theory and the Problem of Method. *Educational Researcher*, 30(1): 29–33.

López, Nancy, Christopher Erwin, Melissa Binder and Mario Javier Chavez. 2018. Making the Invisible Visible: Advancing Quantitative Methods in Higher Education Using Critical Race Theory and Intersectionality. *Race Ethnicity and Education*, 21(2): 180–207.

Lowery, B. S., Hardin, C. D., and Sinclair, S. 2001. Social Influence Effects on Automatic Racial Prejudice. *Journal of Personality and Social Psychology*, 81(5): 842–855.

Lukachko, Alicia, Mark L Hatzenbuehler and Katherine M Keyes. 2014. Structural racism and Myocardial Infarction in the United States. *Social Science & Medicine*, 103: 42–50.

Lutton, Larry S. 2010. *Qualitative Research Approaches for Public Administration*. NY: Taylor and Francis.

Lynn, Marvin and Laurence Parker. 2006. Critical Race Studies in Education: Examining a Decade of Research on U.S. Schools. *The Urban Review*, 38 (4): 257–290.

Manglitz, Elaine, Talmadge C. Guy and Lisa R. Merriweather Hunn. 2006. Using Counter Narratives to Construct a Aialogue on Race, Positionality, and Authority: A Research Tool. Paper presented at the annual Standing

Conference on University Teaching and Research in the Education of Adults (SCUTREA), July 4–6, Trinity and All Saints College, Leeds, UK, www .leeds.ac.uk/educol/documents/155304.htm, accessed December 17, 2020.

Martin, Joanne. 2003. Feminist Theory and Critical Theory: Unexplored Synergies. In Mats Alvesson and Hugh Willmott (eds.), *Studying Management Critically*. London: Sage Publications, pp. 66–91.

Massey, Douglas S. and Nancy A. Denton. 1988. The Dimensions of Residential Segregation. *Social Forces*, 67(2): 281–315.

Matsuda, Mari J., Charles R. Lawrence III, Richard Delgado, Kimberlé Williams Crenshaw. 1993. *Words That Wound: Critical Race Theory, Assaultive Speech, and the First Amendment*. New York: Taylor and Francis.

Matsuda Mari J. 1991. Beside My Sister, Facing the Enemy: Legal Theory Out of Coalition. *Stanford Law Review*, 43(6): 1183–1192.

Matsuda, Mari J. 1987. Looking To The Bottom: Critical Legal Studies and Reparations. *Harvard Civil Rights-Civil Liberties Law Review*, 22(2): 323–399.

Matthews, Peter and Chris Poyner Chris. 2020. Achieving Equality in Progressive Contexts: Queer(Y)Ing Public Administration. *Public Administration Quarterly*, 44 (4), pp. 545–577.

McClain, Paula D., Gloria Y. A. Ayee, Taneisha N. Means, Alicia M. Reyes-Barriéntez and Nura A. Sediqe. 2016. Race, power, and knowledge: tracing the roots of exclusion in the development of political science in the United States. *Politics, Groups, and Identities*, 4(3): 467–482.

McGregor, Alecia. 2016. Politics, Police Accountability, and Public Health: Civilian Review in Newark, New Jersey. *Journal of Urban Health*, 93 (Suppl 1): 141–153.

Merritt, Cullen C. 2020. Invited Essay. *Management Matters*, 18(2), 4. The Public Management Research Association Newsletter, http://pmranet.org/wp-con tent/uploads/Management-Matters-V-18-2.pdf, accessed January 18, 2021.

Mohai, Paul and Bunyan Bryant. 1992. Environmental Racism: Reviewing the Evidence. In Bryant and Mohai (eds), *Race and the Incidence of Environmental Hazards: A Time for Discourse*. Boulder, CO: Westview, 163–176.

Mohai, Paul, David Pellow and J. Timmons Roberts. 2009. Environmental Justice. *Annual Review of Environment and Resources*, 34(1): 405–430.

Moore, Sharon E., Michael A. Robinson, Dewey M. Clayton, A. Christson Adedoyin, Daniel A. Boamah, Eric Kyere, and Dana K. Harmon. 2018. A Critical Race Perspective of Police Shooting of Unharmed Black Males in the United States: Implications for Social Work. *Urban Social Work*, 2 (1): 33–47.

Naylor, Lorenda A., Heather Wyatt-Nichol and Samuel L. Brown. 2015. Inequality: Underrepresentation of African American Males in U. S. Higher Education. *Journal of Public Affairs Education*, 21(4): 523–538.

Neitzel, Jennifer. 2018. Research to practice: understanding the role of implicit bias in early childhood disciplinary practices. *Journal of Early Childhood Teacher Education*, 39(3): 232–242.

Nowak, David J., Satoshi Hirabayashi, Allison Bodine, Eric Greenfield. 2014. Tree and forest effects on air quality and human health in the United States. *Environmental Pollution*, 193: 119–129.

Oakley, Ann (1998). Science, Gender, and Women's Liberation: An Argument Against Postmodernism. *Women's Studies International Forum*, 21 (2):133–146.

Omi, Michael and Howard Winant. 2015. 3rd ed. *Racial Formation in the United States*. New York: Routledge.

Pager, Devah. 2007. *Marked: Race, Crime, and Finding Work in an Era of Mass Incarceration*. Chicago: University of Chicago Press.

Parker, Laurence. 1998. 'Race Is Race Ain't': An Exploration of the Utility of Critical Race Theory in Qualitative Research in Education. *International Journal of Qualitative Studies in Education*, 11(1): 43–55.

Parker, Laurence, Donna Deyhle and Sofia Villenas (eds.). 2019. *Race Is . . . Race Isn't: Critical Race Theory And Qualitative Studies in Education*. NY: Routledge, first edition published in 1999.

Pauli, Benjamin J. 2019. Flint Fights Back: Environmental Justice and Democracy in the Flint Water Crisis. Cambridge, MA: MIT Press.

Pendall, Rolf. 2000. Local Land-Use Regulation and the Chain of Exclusion. *Journal of the American Planning Association*, 66(2): 125–142.

Pew Research Center. 2019. Smartphones help blacks, Hispanics bridge some – but not all – digital gaps with whites. August 20. www.pewresearch.org/ fact-tank/2019/08/20/smartphones-help-blacks-hispanics-bridge-some-but-not-all-digital-gaps-with-whites/, accessed February 2, 2021.

Plessy v. *Ferguson*, 163 U.S. 537 (1896).

Portillo, Shannon. 2020. Invited Essay. *Management Matters*, 18(2), 4. The Public Management Research Association Newsletter, http://pmranet.org/wp-con tent/uploads/Management-Matters-V-18-2.pdf, accessed January 18, 2021.

Portillo, Shannon, Domonic Bearfield and Nicole Humphrey. 2020. The Myth of Bureaucratic Neutrality: Institutionalized Inequity in Local Government Hiring. *Review of Public Personnel Administration*, 40(3) 516–531.

Portillo, Shannon and Nicole Humphrey. 2018. Institutionalism and Assumptions: Institutionalizing Race and Gender in Public Administration

Scholarship. In E. C. Stazyk and H. G. Frederickson (eds.), *Handbook of American Public Administration*, Northampton, MA: Edward Elgar, pp. 289–303.

Pugh, Ann. 1990. My Statistics and Feminism. In Liz Stanley (ed.), *Feminist Praxis*, London: Routledge, pp. 103–113.

Pulido, Laura. 2016. Flint, Environmental Racism, and Racial Capitalism. *Capitalism Nature Socialism*, 27(3): 1–16.

Pulido, Laura. 2000. Rethinking Environmental Racism: White Privilege and Urban Development in Southern California. *Annals of the Association of American Geographers*, 90(1): 12–40.

Pullen, Alison, Sheena Vachhani, Suzanne Gagnon and Nelarine Cornelius. 2017. Editorial: Critical Diversity, Philosophy and Praxis. *Gender, Work and Organization*, 24(5): 451–456.

Office of Management and Budget (OMB) Memorandum, M-20-34. 2020. Memorandum For The Heads Of Executive Departments And Agencies. Executive Office of the President. September 4. www.whitehouse.gov/wp-content/uploads/2020/09/M-20-34.pdf, accessed June 15, 2021.

Orelus, Pierre W. 2010. Black Masculinity under White Supremacy: Exploring the Intersection between Black Masculinity, Slavery, Racism, Heterosexism, and Social Class. *Counterpoints*, 351: 63–111.

Quillin, John M. 2016. Lifestyle Risk Factors Among People Who Have Had Cancer Genetic Testing. *Journal of Genetic Counseling*, 25(5): 957–964.

Raadschelders, Jos C. N. 2011. *Public Administration: The Interdisciplinary Study of Government*. Oxford: Oxford University Press.

Ray, Victor. 2019a. A Theory of Racialized Organizations. *American Sociological Review*, 84(1): 26–53.

Ray, Victor. 2019b. What Is a Racialized Organization? Work in Progress, June 26. www.wipsociology.org/2019/06/26/what-is-a-racialized-organ ization/, accessed January 25, 2021.

Ray, Victor Erik, Antonia Randolph, Megan Underhill and David Luke. 2017. Critical Race Theory, Afro-Pessimism, and Racial Progress Narratives. *Sociology of Race and Ethnicity*, 3(2): 147–158.

Ray, Victor and Louise Seamster. 2016. Rethinking Racial Progress: A Response to Wimmer. *Ethnic and Racial Studies*, 39(8):1361–69.

Reinharz, Shulamit. 1992. *Feminist Methods in Social Research*. Oxford: Oxford University Press.

Rengifo, Andres F. and Morgan Pater. 2017. Close Call: Race and Gender in Encounters with the Police by Black and Latino/a Youth in New York City. *Sociological Inquiry*, 87(2): 337–361.

Rho'Dess, Todd. 2011. From Hope to Change? Obama's 2008 Deracialized Campaign in the Context of the African American Struggle. *Race, Gender & Class*, 18(3/4): 110–122.

Riccucci, Norma M. 2021. Applying Critical Race Theory to Public Administration Scholarship. *Perspectives in Public Management and Governance*, 4(4): 324–338

Riccucci, Norma M. 2010. *Public Administration: Traditions of Inquiry and Philosophies of Knowledge*. Washington, D.C.: Georgetown University Press (2nd edition forthcoming).

Rich, Wilbur C. (ed.) 2007. *African American Perspectives on Political Science*. Philadelphia: Temple University Press.

Richter, Lauren. 2018. Constructing Insignificance: Critical Race Perspectives on Institutional Failure in Environmental Justice Communities. *Environmental Sociology*, 4(1): 107–121.

Ringquist, Evan J. 2005. Assessing Evidence of Environmental Inequities: A Meta-Analysis. *Journal of Policy Analysis and Management*, 24(2): 223–247.

Roberts, Helen. 1981. *Doing Feminist Research*. London: Routledge & Kegan Paul.

Roberts, M. C., Taber, J. M., and Klein, W. M. (2018). Engagement with Genetic Information and Uptake of Genetic Testing: The Role of Trust and Personal Cancer History. *Journal of Cancer Education*, 33(4): 893–900.

Romero, Mary. 2008. Crossing the Immigration and Race Border: A Critical Race Theory Approach To Immigration Studies. *Contemporary Justice Review*, 11(1): 23–37.

Romero, Mary. 2001. State Violence, and the Social and Legal Construction of Latino Criminality: From El Bandido to Gang Member. *Denver University Law Review*,78, 1089–1127.

Ross, K., Stoler, J., and Carcioppolo, N. (2018). The relationship between low perceived numeracy and cancer knowledge, beliefs, and affect. *PLoS One*, 13(6): e0198992. https://doi.org/10.1371/journal.pone.0198992.

Rothwell, Jonathan and Douglas S. Massey. 2009. The Effect of Density Zoning on Racial Segregation in U.S. Urban Areas. *Urban Affairs Review*, 44(6): 779–806.

Sablan, Jenna R. 2019. Can You Really Measure That? Combining Critical Race Theory and Quantitative Methods. *American Educational Research Journal*, 56(1):178–203.

Schneider Christopher. 2003. Integrating Critical Race Theory and Postmodernism: Implications of Race, Class and Gender. *Critical Criminology*, 12(1): 87–103.

Sementelli, Arthur J. and Charles F. Abel. 2000. Recasting Critical Theory: Veblen, Deconstruction, and the Theory-Praxis Gap. *Administrative Theory & Praxis*, 22(3): 458–478.

Shields, A. E., Burke, W., and Levy, D. E. 2008. Differential Use of Available Genetic Tests among Primary Care Physicians in the United States: Results of a National Survey. *Genetics in Medicine*, 10(6): 404–414.

Shields, Patricia M. 2006. Democracy and the Social Feminist Ethics of Jane Addams: A Vision for Public Administration. *Administrative Theory & Praxis*, 28(3): 418–443.

Shields, Patricia M. 2005. Classical Pragmatism: Roots and Promise for a PA Feminist Theory. *Administrative Theory and Praxis*, 27(2): 370–376.

Shields, Patricia M. and Joseph Soeters. 2017. Peaceweaving: Jane Addams, Positive Peace, and Public Administration. *American Review of Public Administration*, 47(3): 323–339.

Siegel, Michael. 2020. Racial Disparities in Fatal Police Shootings: An Empirical Analysis Informed by Critical Race Theory. *Boston University Law Review*, 100: 1069–1092.

Smith, Linda Tuhiwai. 2012. *Decolonizing Methodologies: Research and Indigenous Peoples*. 2nd ed. New York, NY: Zed Books.

Smith, Robert C. 2018. *Hanes Walton, Jr.: Architect of the Black Science of Politics*. Switzerland: Palgrave Macmillan.

Smith-Maddox, Renée and Daniel G. Solórzano. 2002. Using Critical Race Theory, Paulo Freire's Problem-Posing Method, and Case Study Research to Confront Race and Racism in Education. *Qualitative Inquiry*, 8(1): 66–84.

Solórzano, Daniel G. and Tara J. Yosso. 2002. Critical Race Methodology: Counter-Storytelling as an Analytical Framework for Education Research. *Qualitative Inquiry*, 8(1): 23–44.

Solórzano, Daniel G., Miguel Ceja and Tara J. Yosso. 2000. Critical Race Theory, Racial Microaggressions and Campus Racial Climate: The Experiences of African American College Students. *The Journal of Negro Education*, 69(1/2): 60–73.

Stivers, Camilla. 2002. *Gender Images in Public Administration: Legitimacy and the Administrative State*. 2nd ed. Thousand Oaks: Sage.

Stivers, Camilla. 2000. *Bureau Men, Settlement Women: Constructing Public Administration in the Progressive Era*. Lawrence, Kansas: University of Kansas Press.

Stivers, Camilla. 1991. Toward a Feminist Perspective in Public Administration Theory. *Women & Politics*, 10(4): 49–65.

Sue, Derald Wing. *Microaggressions in Everyday Life: Race, Gender, and Sexual Orientation*. Hoboken, NJ: John Wiley & Sons, 2010.

Sung, Kenzo K. and Natoya Coleman. 2019. Framing Critical Race Theory and Methodologies. In Kamden K. Strunk and Leslie Ann Locke (eds.), *Research Methods for Social Justice and Equity in Education*. Cham, Switzerland: Palgrave Macmillan, pp. 45–58.

Swan, Elaine. 2017. What are White People to Do? Listening, Challenging Ignorance, Generous Encounters and the 'Not Yet' as Diversity Research Praxis. *Gender, Work and Organization*, 24(5): 547–563.

Taylor, Jami Kathleen. 2007. Transgender Identities and Public Policy in the United States: The Relevance for Public Administration. *Administration & Society*, 39(7): 833–885.

Torres, Lucas, Mark W. Driscoll and Anthony L. Burrow. 2010. Racial Microaggressions and Psychological Functioning Among Highly Achieving African-Americans: A Mixed-Methods Approach. *Journal of Social and Clinical Psychology*, 29(10): 1074–1099.

Trochmann, Maren B., Shilpa Viswanath, Stephanie Puello and Samantha June Larson. 2021. Resistance or reinforcement? A Critical Discourse Analysis of Racism and Anti-Blackness in Public Administration Scholarship. *Administrative Theory & Praxis*, DOI: 10.1080/ 10841806.2021.1918990.

Tyler, Tom and Cheryl J. Wakslak. 2004. Profiling and Police Legitimacy: Procedural Justice, Attributions of Motive, and Acceptance of Police Authority. *Criminology*, 42(2): 253–281.

Van Dusen, Ben and Jayson Nissen. 2020. Associations between learning assistants, passing introductory physics, and equity: A quantitative critical race theory investigation. *Physical Review Physics Education Research*, 16(1): 010117-1 – 010117-15.

Vincent-Ruz, Paulette. QuantCrit Resources. No date.https://micerportal.files .wordpress.com/2020/06/a-14.-vincent-ruz-p.-micer-poster-2020.pdf

Westmarland, Nicole. 2001. The Quantitative/Qualitative Debate and Feminist Research: A Subjective View of Objectivity. *Forum: Qualitative Social Research*, 2 (1):online. https://webcache.googleusercontent.com/search? q=cache:tYyrYl93t0EJ:www.qualitative-research.net/index.php/fqs/art icle/view/974/2124+&cd=3&hl=en&ct=clnk&gl=us&client=firefox- b-1-d, accessed December 17, 2020.

Wiggershaus, Rolf. 1994. *The Frankfurt School: Its History, Theories, and Political Significance*. Cambridge, MA: MIT Press (translated by Michael Robertson).

Williams, David R. and Salina A. Mohammed. 2013. Racism and Health I: Pathways and Scientific Evidence. *American Behavioral Scientist*, 57(8): 1152–1173.

Williams, David R., Jourdyn A. Lawrence and Brigette A. Davis. 2019. Racism and Health: Evidence and Needed Research. *Annual Review of Public Health*, 40(1): 105–125.

Williams, Monnica T., Matthew D. Skinta, Jonathan W. Kanter, Renée Martin-Willett, Judy Mier-Chairez, Marlena Debreaux and Daniel C. Rosen. 2020. A Qualitative Study of Microaggressions against African Americans on Predominantly White Campuses. BioMed Central, *BMC Psychology*, 8 (111): 1–13.

Williams, Patricia J. 1991. *Alchemy of Race and Rights: Diary of a Law Professor*. Cambridge: Harvard University Press.

Williams, Patricia J., 1987. Alchemical Notes: Reconstructing Ideals from Deconstructed Rights." *Harvard Civil Rights – Civil Liberties Law Review* 401.

Wilson, Woodrow. 1887. The Study of Public Administration. *Political Science Quarterly*, 2(2): 197–222.

Witt, Matthew T. 2006. Notes from the Margin: Race, Relevance, and the Making of Public Administration. *Administrative Theory and Praxis*, 28 (1): 36–68.

Wittenbrink, B., Judd, C. M., & Park, B. 2001. Spontaneous Prejudice in Context: Variability in Automatically Activated Attitudes. *Journal of Personality and Social Psychology*, 81(5): 815–827.

Wolfson, Andrew. 2020. Kentucky's self-defense laws negated possible homicide charges in Breonna Taylor's death. *Louisville Courier Journal*. September 23. www.courier-journal.com/story/news/local/breonna-taylor/2020/09/23/end-case-went-down-just-experts-criminal-law-predicted-none-three-officers-involved-death-breonna-ta/5864466002/, accessed January 5, 2021.

Woodard, Maurice and Michael B. Preston. 1985. Black Political Scientists: Where Are the New Ph.D.s? *PS: Political Science & Politics*, 18(1): 80–88.

Wright James E. II and Andrea M. Headley. 2021. Can Technology Work for Policing? Citizen Perceptions of Police-Body Worn Cameras. *American Review of Public Administration*, 51(1): 17–27.

Wright, James E. II and Andrea M. Headley. 2020. Police Use of Force Interactions: Is Race Relevant or Gender Germane? *American Review of Public Administration*, 50(8): 851–864.

Wright, James E. II and Cullen C. Merritt. 2020. Social Equity and COVID-19: The Case of African Americans. *Public Administration Review*, 80(5): 820–826.

Zuberi, Tukufu. 2001. *Thicker than Blood: How Racial Statistics Lie*. Minneapolis: University of Minnesota Press.

Zuberi, Tukufu. 2000. Deracializing Social Statistics: Problems in the Quantification of Race. *Annals of the American Academy of Political and Social Science*, 568(March): 172–185.

Zuberi, Tukufu and Eduardo Bonilla-Silva. 2008. *White Logic, White Methods: Racism and Methodology*. Lanham, MD: Rowan & Littlefield.

Acknowledgment

This essay draws from my Herbert Simon Award Lecture delivered to the Midwest Political Science Association in April of 2021. I gratefully acknowledge the Midwest Public Administration Caucus, William Resh and the 2021 Herbert Simon Award selection committee, Professors Charles Shipan, Mona Vakilifathi, and Elizabeth Bell, as well as the professor who anonymously nominated me.

Cambridge Elements ☰

Public and Nonprofit Administration

Andrew Whitford
University of Georgia
Andrew Whitford is Alexander M. Crenshaw Professor of Public Policy in the School of Public and International Affairs at the University of Georgia. His research centers on strategy and innovation in public policy and organization studies.

Robert Christensen
Brigham Young University
Robert Christensen is professor and George Romney Research Fellow in the Marriott School at Brigham Young University. His research focuses on prosocial and antisocial behaviors and attitudes in public and nonprofit organizations.

About the Series
The foundation of this series are cutting-edge contributions on emerging topics and definitive reviews of keystone topics in public and nonprofit administration, especially those that lack longer treatment in textbook or other formats. Among keystone topics of interest for scholars and practitioners of public and nonprofit administration, it covers public management, public budgeting and finance, nonprofit studies, and the interstitial space between the public and nonprofit sectors, along with theoretical and methodological contributions, including quantitative, qualitative and mixed-methods pieces.

The Public Management Research Association
The Public Management Research Association improves public governance by advancing research on public organizations, strengthening links among interdisciplinary scholars, and furthering professional and academic opportunities in public management.

Cambridge Elements $\equiv$

Public and Nonprofit Administration

Printed in the United States
by Baker & Taylor Publisher Services